The Kids' Catalog of Passover

The Kids' Catalog
of Passover

A WORLDWIDE CELEBRATION OF STORIES, SONGS, CUSTOMS, CRAFTS, FOOD, AND FUN

Barbara Rush
Cherie Karo Schwartz

The Jewish Publication Society
Philadelphia
2000 • 5760

Design and composition by Elizabeth Anne O'Donnell

Manufactured in the United States of America

09 08 07 06 05 04 03 02 01   10 9 8 7 6 5 4 3 2

Library of Congress Cataloging-in-Publication Data

Rush, Barbara.
    The kids' catalog of Passover : a worldwide celebration : stories, songs, customs, crafts, food, and fun from around the world / Barbara Rush and Cherie Karo Schwartz. — 1st ed.
        p.   cm.
    Includes bibliographical references and index.
    Summary: Presents stories, songs, crafts, recipes, games, and more related to various aspects of the celebration of the Jewish holiday of Passover.
    ISBN 0-8276-0687-7
    1. Passover Juvenile literature. 2. Seder Juvenile literature. [1. Passover.
2. Seder.] I. Schwartz, Cherie Karo. II. Title.
BM695.P3R87 1999
    296.4'37—dc21   99-35118
                                                                          CIP

The authors and the publisher gratefully acknowledge permission to include the following: "Symbols of Spring" pen and ink drawing © by Tsila Schwartz; "Baby Moses," "History," and "Wandering" original music © by Fran Avni; "Miriam's Slow Snake Dance by the Riverside" original music © by Linda Hirschhorn; "Miriam" rubber stamp © by Barbara Lehman, Lehman Design; "Illuminated Letter 'Pey'" © by Lisa Rauchwerger, Cutting Edge Creations; opening art for Parts 1, 2, 3, and 4 © by Judy Lande Haran; Eisenstein *Haggadah* illustrations © by Hebrew Publishing Company.

The border on the title page was reprinted from the Venice *Haggadah*, Italy, 1792.

*The publication of this book
was assisted through a generous grant
from the MAURICE AMADO FOUNDATION,
whose mission is to perpetuate
Sephardic heritage and culture.*

We dedicate this book, with love and gratitude,
to our wonderful husbands, Don Rush and Larry Schwartz,
who breathed every word and every image
of the manuscript with us.

Contents

Introduction   xvi
How to Use This Book   xviii
A Special Note for Adults   xix
Notes from the Publisher   xx
A Mini-Dictionary   xxi
Jews around the World: Celebrating an Ancient
*   Holiday   xxii*

Part 1
Maggid: Telling the Story   2

1 *The Exodus*   Introduction   4
Story   4   Story: "From Slavery to Freedom"   4
                    Craft: A Life-Size Exodus Mural   8
                    Songs: "Baby Moses" by Fran Avni; "An Exodus Rap"   10
                    Stories from the Rabbis: "Miriam's Dream"; "Moses and the
                        Coals"; "How Did Moses Find Out That He Was Jewish?";
                        "Taking the First Step"   11
                    Seder Talk: Taking Risks   13
                    Custom: Fruits from the Sea   13
                    Fun: Play a Game; Take a Nature Walk; Plant a Parsley and
                        Radish Garden; Create a Family Spring Poem   14
                    A Seder Reading   16
                    More Seder Talk: Blessing for the Land   17
                    More Fun: An Extra-Hard Riddle   17

2 *The Ten Plagues*   18   Introduction   18
                    Story: "Frogs and More Frogs"   18
                    Crafts: A Froggy Critter; A Plague of Puppets   20

Fun: Scrambled Plagues; An Interview with Pharaoh   25
Customs: Ten Drops of Wine; Bowl of Wine
    (from Morocco)   26
Seder Talk: What Are Some New Plagues in Our World?   27

Introduction   28
Story: "Miriam and Her Tambourine"   28
Fun: Create a Story   30
Craft: Miriam's Tambourine   31
Song: "Miriam's Slow Snake Dance by the Riverside" by Linda
    Hirschhorn   31
Custom: A Cup for Miriam   35
More Fun: A Bowl for Miriam   35
Seder Readings: Remembering the Women; How the Women
    Came Dancing   36
Seder Talk: A Difficult Question about the Midwives   37

3 Miriam and the Women   28

Introduction   38
Story: "The Children Are the Future" by Rachel Sara
    Petroff   38
Craft: A Freedom Banner   42
Songs: "Hymn of the Partisans"; "Wandering" by Fran Avni;
    "Avadim Hayinu"   43
Seder Talk: What Does It Mean to Be Free?; Freedom
    Wishes   46
Custom: *B'ivhilut* (from Morocco)   46
More Seder Talk: ASL—Another Way to Say "Freedom";
    Showing That We Are Free   47
A Seder Reading: We Were Slaves   48
Project: A Seder for Everyone   48

4 Freedom for All   38

Part 2
Preparing for the Seder 50

5 *Getting Ready* **52**

Introduction 52
Story: "A Letter to God" (from Iran) 52
Before-Seder Talk: Who Will Come to Your Seder? 54
Craft: A Seder Invitation 55
Rules: What Is *Chametz?* 56
Customs: Searching for *Chametz*, An *Afikoman* Dustpan
   (from France) 58
Project: Spring Cleaning *Tzedakah* 58
Seder Talk: Getting Rid of the *Chametz* in Our Lives 59
Fun: A Special *Chametz* Riddle 59

6 *The Haggadah* **60**

Introduction 60
Story: "The *Haggadah* That Traveled" by Fred Hertz (from
   Germany) 60
Seder Talk: Where Does the Word *Haggadah* Come From?;
   Who Reads the *Haggadah?*; The Oldest *Haggadah;* A
   Haggadah for the Blind 62
Song: "History" by Fran Avni 65
Craft: Illuminated Page of a *Haggadah* 66
More Seder Talk: Where is Moses Mentioned in the
   Haggadah? 67

7 *The Seder and the Seder Plate* **68**

Introduction 68
Story: "Radishes for the Seder" (from Spain) 68
Blessings 72
Seder Talk: Other Hebrew Words that Sound Like "Seder" 73
The Order of the Seder 73
Custom: How Many Seders Are There? 74

The Symbols of the Seder Plate   74

  Karpas, the Green Vegetable   74

  Karpas Customs: *Karpas* around the World   74

  Karpas Snacks   75

  Maror, the Bitter Herb   75

  Maror Customs: Four Special *Maror* Traditions; Still More
    Maror Customs   75

  Charoses or *Charoset,* the Sweet Mortar   76

  Charoset Seder Talk: Why Is There No Blessing for the
    Charoset? Why Is *Charoset* Sweet?   76

  Five Favorite *Charoset* Recipes: Barbara's *Charoses;*
    Cherie's *Charoses;* Danielle's *Charoset;* Seemah Mares's
    Charoset (from Rangoon); A *Charoset* Pyramid   77

  Fun: A Nut Game   81

  Zeroa, the Shankbone as a Reminder of Sacrifice   82

  Zeroa Seder Talk: Three Questions   82

  Zeroa Custom: Keeping the Bone All Year (from
    Afghanistan)   83

  More *Zeroa* Seder Talk: The Shankbone Is a Reminder of
    the "Outstretched Arm" of God   82

  Betzah, the Egg for New Life   83

  Betzah Customs: Four Egg Traditions   83

  Betzah Recipe: Red Eggs (from the Sephardic
    tradition)   83

Seder Talk: Seder Plate Symbols   84

Custom: No Seder Plate! (from Yemen and the Caucasus
  Mountains)   84

Poem: The Seder Plate Checklist   85

Crafts: A Stenciled Seder Plate Symbols Tablecloth; A *Hamsa*
  (or Hand) Seder Plate   85

8 Lots of Matzah   90

Introduction   90

Story: "The *Matzah* Cover that Saved a Life" (from Syria)   92

Craft: An Iron-on *Matzah* Cover   95

Recipe: Make Your Own *Matzah*   96

Seder Talk: Did *Matzah* Always Look the Way It Does
   Now?   97

Fun: Four *Matzah* Riddles   97

Customs: *Matzah* on Your Head (from Europe); *Matzah* for
   Everyone   98

Project: How Can You Share *Matzah* with Others?   99

More Customs: Four Ways to Break the Middle *Matzah;* Four
   Ways to Hide the *Afikoman*   99

A New Custom: The *Matzah* of Hope   101

Part 3
At the Seder   102

9 *Asking*
Questions   *104*

Introduction   104

Story: "Passover Clothing in Chelm"   104

Customs: May You Live to 120!; New Clothing for
   Passover   106

Fun: Something New for Your Seder   108

The Four Questions: Why Is This Night Different?   108

More Customs: What Are Some Different Ways to Ask the
   Four Questions?   110

Song: *"Mah Nishtanah"*   111

Seder Talk: How Have the Four Questions Changed Over the
   Years?   112

Craft: The "Four Questions" *Kippah*   113

More Fun: Find Other "Fours" in the Seder; Be A Seder
   Detective   113

More Seder Talk: The Four Sons; How Are We Like the Four
  Sons? 114
Yet Another Custom: Four or Five Cups of Wine? 115

Introduction 116
Story: *"Dayenu"* (from Poland and Tunisia) 116
Song: *"Dayeinu"* 120
Fun: A New *"Dayenu"*; And Another *"Dayenu"* 121
Craft: A Micrography Picture 122
Custom: A Persian Scallion "Battle" 123

10 *Dayenu!* **116**

Introduction 124
Story: "Hershele's Passover Feast" 125
Customs: What Do Jews Eat at Their Seders? 128
Ashkenazic Recipe: *Knaidlach* or *Matzo* Balls 128
Customs: Floaters or Sinkers?; Favorite Sephardic Seder
  Foods 130
Sephardic Recipes: Italian Rice Soup; Moroccan Green
  Soup 131
Still More Customs: More about Passover Foods 133
Cherie's and Barbara's Favorite Family Recipes: Spicy
  Eggplant; Sweet Israel Chicken; Passover Almond Cake;
  Forgotten Cookie Clouds 134
Fun: A Garbage Garden 140
Seder Talk: Passover Memories 141

11 *The Festive
Meal* **124**

Introduction 142
Story: "Elijah's Passover Return" 142
Craft: An *Afikoman* Bag 146
Customs: Four *Afikoman* Questions 147
Seder Talk: Making Things Whole 148
Poem: "The Great *Afikoman* Search" 149
Birkat Hamazon: Saying Grace after the Meal 151

12 *The Afikoman* **142**

Part 4
Singing Praises and Concluding the Seder   152

13 *Elijah the Prophet* **154**

Introduction   154
Story: "The Treasured Cup of Elijah" (from the Ukraine)   155
Customs: Welcoming Elijah; The Cup of Elijah; A Chair for
    Elijah   158
Song: *"Eliyahu Hanavi"* ("Elijah's Song")   159
Seder Talk: Opening the Door   160
Fun: Elijah Buddies   160
Crafts: Elijah's Cup; A Clay Elijah's Cup; Welcome Blessing
    Placemat   161
More Seder Talk: *Hallel*   163

14 *Some Newer Exoduses* **164**

Introduction   164
Story: "An Exodus Story: A Tale from Ethiopia"   164
Crafts: Clay Figures; Immigration Tiles   167
Seder Talk: Other Exoduses to *Eretz Yisrael*   167
Immigration Stories: From Yemen; From Egypt; From
    Romania; From Poland   169
Projects: Gathering Family Stories; Family Treasures   171
Craft: Immigration Bookmarks   174

Introduction 176

Story: "Jerusalem's Secret" 177

Fun: Israeli Pen Pals; A Bar/Bat Mitzvah Trip to Israel; Plan an
Israel Exhibit 178

Crafts: A Jerusalem Puzzle; A Papercut *Mizrach* 180

Seder Talk: Next Year in Jerusalem 182

Project: A Prayer for Jerusalem 182

Song: *"L'shanah Haba-ah Biy'rushalayim"* 183

15 *Next Year in Jerusalem* 176

Introduction 184

Songs: *"Adir Hu"*; *"Echad Mi Yodei-a"* (Hebrew) and *"Quen
Supiese"* (Ladino); *"Chad Gadya"* (Hebrew) and *"Un
Cavritico"* (Ladino) 184

Craft: A *Chad Gadya* Glove 191

Customs: Happy Passover; After the Seder: Beating the Water;
More *Matzo;* Visiting Friends; Maimuna 192

Seder Talk: Ending the Seder; Song: "Lo Yisa Goy" 193

A Final Seder Question: How Can We Make a Good Start for
the Next Year? 195

Fun: A Last Detective Test 196

Your Ideas for Your Next Seder 197

16 *Ending with Praises and Songs* 184

More about Passover: *Fun-filled Books, Tapes,
and Videos* 198

Notes on Sources 204

Haggadot Used in This Book 206

Bibliography 208

Acknowledgments 210

Index 216

Introduction

Do you know what is new and old at the same time? The *Haggadah* (**ha-gahd-DAH** or **hah-GUHD-duh**)! It's old because it retells the story of the Exodus from Egypt, which took place more than three thousand years ago. Jews have been retelling the same story for thousands of years, every year, at Passover seders all over the world, just as you are preparing to tell the story at your seder!

We reread the *Haggadah* each year because the Torah tells us—not once, not twice, not three times, but *four* times—that we must tell the story to our children so that we may remember the years of slavery and savor the taste of freedom, and so that our children may tell it to their children. But do you think the story can be told and retold all these years without changing even a little bit? Of course not! Every year, as new family and friends join in the celebration, the story is given new life, thanks to the new questions, new recipes, new prayers, and new hopes that each new generation brings to the seder table. That is why the *Haggadah* is new and old at the same time.

This year it is *your* turn to tell the story. The seder belongs to *you*. How can *you* retell the old story in a new way? Turn through the pages of this book, discover new stories, new customs, new ways of understanding an "old" story, and decide how you would like to tell the story anew. It's *your* seder. How can you help your family and friends retell

the Passover story? How can you best celebrate this holiday of freedom?

We hope that you, like us, come to love Passover. It has always been—and still is—our favorite Jewish holiday. Cherie remembers the sound of hazelnuts rolling down the wood floors while she played the nut games with her family. Barbara's favorite seder at a *kibbutz* in Israel included more than two thousand people! Children danced and sang and played musical instruments to celebrate the coming of spring.

We wrote this book to share our favorite stories, recipes, and the many holiday customs that we've always loved, as well as the new ones that we've discovered and added each year to our own seders. To help us write this book, many of our friends shared their family traditions from all over the world and helped us create many new celebrations!

So, you see, this book has many old customs from our tradition, and it has many new stories, songs, recipes, crafts, riddles, games, and ideas to discuss, too. Choose from them all. Add customs and foods from Jews of other countries to your seder! And enjoy feeling yourself connected to your enormous family of Jews all over the world!

Happy Passover!

How to Use This Book

Passover is a time for asking questions. In the spirit of Passover, this book is filled with many questions. For instance, did you know that the number four appears many times during the seder? How many times? Well, there are four questions, four sons, four cups of wine. (Can you find any other times when the number four is mentioned?) That is why we have decided to divide our book into four sections:

1. *Maggid*: Telling the Story
2. Preparing for the Seder
3. At the Seder
4. Singing Praises and Concluding the Seder

You'll notice that each section has four parts! That means it contains stories, crafts, and lots of other things in groups of four!

You will probably read most of this book before the seder. Share some of the ideas with the rest of your family—including your brothers and sisters—and friends! Then decide what to add to your own seder. If you are going to a seder at someone else's house, you may want to bring some of the stories, songs, crafts, or ideas to share with them. Wouldn't that be a wonderful seder gift?

Don't worry if you don't have time to read every story or sing every song in the book this year. Save them for next year. If you have your own ideas about new customs (*minhagim:* **minn-hah-GEEHM**) or stories, write them down on the blank page at the end of this book. In that way, this book will serve as your seder "guide" for many, many years.

A Special Note for Adults

**"And you will tell it to your children,
that they should remember. . . ."**

These are the words in the *Haggadah* that we read every Passover, and which serve as the cornerstone for this book. We hope you'll find in these pages a tapestry of stories, songs, customs, crafts, recipes, and projects created especially for children to share with their families and friends as they prepare for the Passover seders.

How can you help your children retell the Passover story? First, you can help them make the connection between the treasure trove of ideas in this book and your own family's Passover celebration. Second, you can help your children see the modern yet timeless beauty of this most celebrated of all holidays, to sense and feel part of *K'lal Yisrael,* the worldwide community of Jewish people. You might introduce into your seder some of the customs of Jews of other lands, or from places where your family has lived or visited. Or you might help others in need of food or freedom. However you choose to use this book, we hope you'll enjoy sharing it with your children for years and years to come.

Notes from the Publisher

A safety note about the crafts in this book:
Some of the crafts in this book call for the use of scissors, needles, or other potentially dangerous tools. Before beginning any craft, get either help or the "go-ahead" from a responsible adult. Read the directions and assemble all the materials you will need before you begin.

A safety note about the recipes in this book:
A kitchen can be a dangerous place. Watch out for splattering oil or boiling water. Some of the recipes in this book are intended only for older children. Before beginning any of the recipes, make sure an adult is available to help. Read the entire recipe and assemble all the ingredients and utensils (pots, pans, spoons, knives, and so forth) before you begin.

A note about the spellings in this book:
There are many ways to spell Hebrew words using the English alphabet. *Afikoman,* for example, is frequently spelled *afikomen.* Some of the music and other items in this book contained different spellings when they were originally published. We use their original spellings for those words, including the use of the underdot to indicate the gutteral "ch" sound. New material, written especially for this book, created a different challenge—because Jews from different parts of the world pronounce Hebrew words differently. For instance, some Jews say "**mat-ZAH**." Others say "**MAT-zo**!" So, which pronunciation (and spelling) is used in this book?

   Since Israel is the only country where Hebrew is the main language, the authors of this book use the Israeli pronunciation for most of the Hebrew material in this book. However, if a word in a custom, recipe, story, poem, or song comes from a *specific* part of the world where the pronunciation of Hebrew words is different from the Israeli pronunciation, the authors use the pronunciation and spelling from that specific place. Where two pronunciations for a Hebrew word are given, the first is the Israeli (Sephardic) pronunciation. For the plural of the Hebrew word "seder," we use the English plural form "seders." In Israel, since there is only one Passover seder, many people rarely or never use the Hebrew plural form.

A Mini-Dictionary

There are several words you should know as we start our Passover journey:

Jews; Hebrews; Israelites; Children of Israel: These are different names for the Jewish people.

Midrash: Midrash (**mihd-RASH** or **MIHD-rahsh**) is a story created to help explain stories in the Bible. In Hebrew, the word looks like this:

מִדְרָשׁ

Mitzrayim; **Egypt:** *Mitzrayim* (**mits-RYE-ihm**) is the Hebrew word for "tight places." It is also the Hebrew word for Egypt. *Mitzrayim* is spelled like this in Hebrew:

מִצְרַיִם

Pesach: Pesach is the Hebrew word for Passover. In Hebrew, the word looks like this:

פֶּסַח

Red Sea; Reed Sea: These are both names of the sea crossed by the Israelites.

Redemption: Redemption means to be set free, to be released. When the Israelites were slaves in ancient Egypt, they had to find a way to be released from slavery. Their redemption consisted of three parts: 1) God saw the Israelites' suffering and came to their aid; 2) Moses led the people to freedom; and 3) the people participated in their own redemption by having faith in God and in Moses' leadership, and by following Moses to freedom.

Torah; Bible: The Torah consists of the first five books of the Bible. The story of the Exodus is told in the second book of the Torah. Torah is spelled like this in Hebrew:

תּוֹרָה

Coby Gould, age 12

Jews around the World:
Celebrating an Ancient Holiday

Here are four questions to start you on your Passover journey:

1. How old is the festival of *Pesach?*
   Answer: It is older than we can count. *Pesach* was a festival that celebrated spring long before the Exodus from Egypt, even before the Children of Israel went to Egypt!

2. Who celebrates Passover?
   Answer: Jews all over the world. Passover is the most widely celebrated of all Jewish holidays.

3. Jews in different parts of the world are known by different names. What are they?
   Answer: There are three different groups (you may need to look at a map to answer this question):

   a) Ashkenazic (or Ashkenazi) Jews—Most Jews whose families came from Eastern Europe, Germany, and France.

   b) Sephardic (or Sephardi) Jews—Most Jews whose families left Spain and Portugal at the end of the 1400s. They went to live in countries around the Mediterranean and Black Seas such as Greece, Italy, Bulgaria, Turkey, and countries in North Africa.

   c) Oriental Jews—Most Jews whose families lived in Kurdistan, Iraq, Iran, and Yemen. Sometimes they are called Sephardic Jews, too.

   d) There are also Jews in India, Pakistan, and other Asian countries, as well as Jews in New Zealand, Australia, South America, South Africa, and other places. And, in our own country, there are even Jews in Alaska and Hawaii.

   Yes, there are Jewish people all around the world.

4. What languages do Jews in different parts of the world speak?
   Answer: Almost all Jews speak the language of the country in which they live. For example, Jews in the United States speak English, while Jews in France speak French, and Jews in Germany speak German. Almost all Jews—no matter where they live—pray

in Hebrew. Our Torah and our prayers are written in Hebrew, and Hebrew is the language of Israel, the homeland of the Jewish people. That's why Jews almost everywhere study Hebrew.

Do you know that Jews usually know one other language besides Hebrew and their native language? It's usually a special Jewish language that combines Hebrew and the language of their country.

Here are examples of four Jewish languages:

a) Jews from Spain speak Ladino, which is Spanish plus Hebrew.

b) Most Jews from Germany speak Yiddish, which is German plus Hebrew.

c) Jews from Persia speak Judeo-Persian, which is Persian plus Hebrew.

d) Many Jews from North Africa speak Judeo-Arabic, which is Arabic plus Hebrew.

You will find some of these languages in this book. (Do you know the special Jewish language in *your* family?)

Judy Lande Haran

Judy Lande Haran

Maggid: Telling the Story

Passover celebrates one of the most important events in Jewish history: our freedom. That's why the Passover story begins with the story of our Exodus from Egypt.

The Bible tells us that the Children of Israel went out of Egypt in the spring. So Passover, of course, is celebrated during the spring. It comes on the fourteenth day of the Hebrew month of *Nisan* (in March or April).

Passover has many names. In Hebrew, the word for Passover is *Pesach*. No one knows what the word *Pesach* really means. Some people say that it comes from the Hebrew word *pasah,* which means "to skip" because God, as you will read in the story, "skipped" over the Jewish houses to save the Jewish firstborn children.

There are at least four names for Passover: Holiday of Spring *(Chag ha Aviv)*, Holiday of Matzah *(Chag ha Matzot)*, Season of Our Freedom *(Zeman Cherutainu*, pronounced **Chey-roo-TAY-noo**), and Holiday of Paschal Offering *(Chag ha Pesach)*.

Each name tells us about a different way of understanding the holiday. Each name emphasizes a different theme. But no matter what name it's called, Passover makes it possible for us to recall this event in Jewish history.

INTRODUCTION

This is the story of the Jews' going out from Mitzrayim, *the place of slavery, into the land of freedom. It is told in the Book of Exodus in the Torah.*

The story of the Exodus begins when the Jewish people first settled in Egypt over three thousand years ago. At that time they were called the Israelites or Hebrews. The first to come was Joseph, the son of Jacob and Rachel. (Jacob was the son of Isaac and Rebecca, and Isaac was the son of Abraham and Sarah, the first Jews.) Joseph's brothers were very jealous of him. They thought that their father, Jacob, loved Joseph more than he loved them. So they threw Joseph into a pit and left him there to die. But Joseph was rescued by traveling merchants who took him to Egypt and sold him as a slave. Joseph was very wise. Soon the Pharaoh **(FAIR-oh)** *heard about his wisdom and invited Joseph to become his advisor in the palace.*

Let us retell the story, just as our ancestors have done from generation to generation.

STORY

From Slavery to Freedom
retold from the Torah

Now one year there was a great famine in Israel. The rain did not fall. Wheat and vegetables could not grow. Many Israelites made the long journey into Egypt to buy food. Among them was Joseph's family. There, in Egypt, Joseph and his family were reunited. After that, many more of the Israelites went to live in Egypt. And it was there, in Egypt, that Joseph died. The Israelites continued to live in peace for many, many generations.

But then there rose a new king over Egypt. He did not know of Joseph's wisdom or the good things that Joseph had done for the Egyptians hundreds of years before. This pharaoh saw the many, many Israelites in his land, and he was

Geismar Haggadah, Germany, 1928

The Exodus Story **1**

afraid they might become too mighty, so he made the lives of the Israelites hard and miserable. He forced them to work long hours in the hot sun, to make bricks, and to build cities. The Israelites had no rest, not even on the Sabbath.

Geismar Haggadah, Germany, 1928

Still Pharaoh was not satisfied. He issued a decree: "All the Hebrew baby boys are to be killed at the moment of their birth." But two Egyptian midwives, Shifrah **(SHIFF-rah)** and Puah **(POO-ah)**, refused to follow Pharaoh's instructions, saying, "We cannot kill the babies." They even tried to fool Pharaoh. They told him, "We don't know when the children are born. The Israelite women give birth by themselves, even before we can help them."

So Pharaoh devised a new plan. "I order all the Hebrew baby boys thrown into the Nile River to drown!"

The Israelites were terrified. "What can we do to save our children?" they cried.

Now, in Egypt there lived a husband and wife, Amram and Yocheved **(yoh-CHEHV-ed)**. Yocheved gave birth to a baby boy and hid him from the Egyptians for three months. Then, when he was too old to hide, she placed him tenderly in a wicker basket and set the basket into the river Nile. Miriam, the baby's sister, stayed close by to watch over him. That day, when Pharaoh's daughter came to bathe in the river, she saw the baby. "Hmm," she thought, "this must be a Hebrew baby." She had pity on the poor baby, so she drew him out of the water. Then Miriam came out of her hiding place and said, "I know a woman who can nurse the baby!" Of course, that woman was Yocheved, their mother! In that way, Miriam made sure that the baby could remain with his mother a little longer. Pharaoh's daughter named him Moses, which means, "I drew him out."

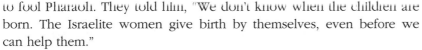

Zak Schwartz, age 17

Geismar Haggadah, Germany, 1928

Moses was raised in Pharaoh's palace. Time passed, and Moses grew into a man. He saw his people, the Israelites, treated badly, and he felt their sorrow. One day Moses saw a taskmaster beating a slave. This was more than he could bear. He killed the taskmaster, and ran far away to a different land called Midian. There he married a woman named Tsipporah and became a shepherd.

Meanwhile, God saw how Moses loved his people. And one day, while Moses was tending his sheep, he suddenly saw a burning bush that did not burn up. What could this be? Moses stepped closer to the flames. Then, just as suddenly, he heard God's voice coming from the bush. "I am God, the God of your ancestors. . . . I have seen how My people are suffering and have come to free them. I will send you to Pharaoh, and you will free My people, the Israelites, from *Mitzrayim.*"

So Moses and his brother Aaron went to Pharaoh, warning of the plagues God would send until Pharaoh set the Israelites free. With each plague, Pharaoh was frightened and decided to let the Israelites go. But each time God removed the plague, Pharaoh changed his mind. There were nine terrible plagues—blood in the Nile River, frogs, lice, wild beasts, cattle disease, boils, hail, locusts, and darkness. Then God sent the tenth plague, the most terrible of all: the killing of the firstborn in every family. All the Israelites were told to mark the doorposts of their houses with the blood of a lamb. Then the Angel of Death would "pass over" their houses without killing the Hebrew children inside. The next morning Pharaoh saw that his own firstborn child had died. He was terribly frightened. Once again he called for Moses. "Take the Israelites out of Egypt!" he cried.

And so the Israelites prepared to leave. They had to leave in a great hurry, so they took only a few possessions—the clothes on their backs and the bread dough that had not had time to rise. And they began their journey.

Hundreds of thousands of Israelites marched out of Egypt toward freedom. God had rescued them from slavery with a mighty hand and an outstretched arm. But Moses was still unsure what to do until God gave him more wondrous signs. During the day there was a pillar of clouds to guide the Israelites through the desert. At night there was a pillar of fire to give light.

But was Pharaoh pleased to see the Israelites leave? No! When he realized the Israelites had fled and that he would not have slaves to do his work, Pharaoh sent his great army after them. Pharaoh's horses and chariots and soldiers raced to catch the slaves, who were at the edge of the Reed Sea, with the water on one side, the armies of Pharaoh on the other. Afraid, they cried out to Moses. God heard their cries and told Moses to hold up his arm over the water. The sea would part!

Crossing the sea.
Livorno Haggadah, Italy, 1867

The Israelites crossed over on dry land in the middle of the sea, but the armies of the Egyptians came right after them. Just then, the walls of water rushed back together, washing over the chariots and horses and soldiers, and they drowned.

On the other side of the river, there was noise and confusion. No one knew what to do. First, Moses and the people sang a song of thanks and praise to God for saving them. And then Miriam picked up her tambourine and slowly began to dance and sing a song to God in thanks for being saved. All the other women took their tambourines and joined Miriam. They sang the song of freedom and they danced to celebrate life. "Now we are free, we are free!" they shouted. And so the Israelites began their forty-year journey through the desert to the land of milk and honey, the Land of Israel.

Stamp made by Barbara Lehman, Lehman Design

Cheryl Rush, age 7

CRAFT

A Life-Size Exodus Mural

Each of us, the *Haggadah* tells us, should feel as if he or she went out of Egypt. Here's a way for you to create a personal mural of your family and seder guests so that you, too, can feel like you're leaving *Mitzrayim*.

> **WHAT YOU NEED:**
>
> very large craft paper (large, standard-sized roll, 3 feet wide)
> a pencil
> scissors
> magic markers in a variety of colors

> **WHAT YOU DO:**

1. Place the paper on the floor.
2. Lie down on your back on the paper while someone traces the outline of your body onto the paper. Then ask the members of your

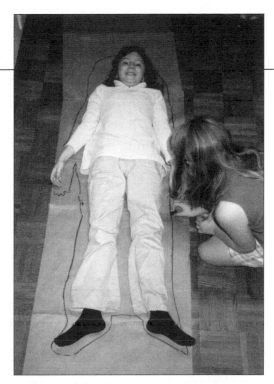

family to lie down on the paper so that you can trace their outlines. Remember to include your pets!

3. Make a large figure for Moses. Maybe an adult could pose as Moses. Moses is shown in many pictures with his staff. What do you think the other people would have been carrying?

4. Cut out the figures.

5. With the magic markers, draw clothes, faces, and hair for your figures. Don't forget Moses' long white beard!

6. Hang the figure of Moses on a wall near your seder table. Then hang the other family figures (and pets!) behind him.

ANOTHER WAY TO DO THIS PROJECT:

1. If you do not have room for such a large-sized project, you can draw all of the figures much smaller on any size of construction paper.

2. Find photographs of your family and friends and tape or glue them at the top of each drawing, instead of drawing their faces!

First ask someone to trace the outline of your body.

Then fill it in with colors.

Katherine Leibel, age 7

SONGS

Baby Moses

Latin feel

Words & Music
Fran Avni

Yo - che - ved was his mo - ther and Mi - ri - am his

sis - ter he was found by Pha - raoh's daugh - ter and brought up as her

son _____ Tell me who _____ was the one _____

__ it was Mo - ses _____ ba - by Mo - ses _____

__ He was found by Pha - raoh's daugh - ter when she pulled him from the

wa - ter she called him Mo - ses _____ ba - by Mo - ses

An Exodus Rap

There are many ways to retell the Exodus story at your seder. Try putting it into a rap, where there is a strong beat and rhythm, like this:

Oh, gather round children
and hear the story
of mighty Pharaoh
and all his glory.

He made the Jews
work night and day.
No time for rest.
No time for play. . . .

Can you finish telling the story, keeping the rhythm and rhyme? Ask the seder guests to help keep time by clapping. Maybe some of the guests can help you make up verses!

STORIES FROM THE RABBIS

You have just read the ancient Exodus story from the Torah. Hundreds of years ago, the Rabbis created more stories to help explain some of the stories in the Torah. These *midrashim* have been retold year after year, each generation handing the stories down to the next generation, just as the stories at your Passover table are retold year after year, from one generation to another. You'll find many of these *midrashim* in the Talmud; some are even in the *Haggadah*. Here are four *midrashim*, which the Rabbis told to help us better understand the Exodus story:

1. Miriam's Dream

Miriam, the sister of Aaron and Moses, had many dreams. When she was only five years old, she dreamed that her parents would give birth to a boy named Moses, and that he would grow up to lead the Israelites to freedom. She believed in this dream so strongly that she convinced her parents to try to have another child, even though they were frightened of giving birth to a baby boy (who would have to be killed according to Pharaoh's harsh decree). When it was time for her mother to give birth, Miriam helped her mother deliver the baby, and

Symbols of spring and earth's bounty.
Tsila Schwartz

helped to weave the basket that would save her brother from drowning in the river.

2. Moses and the Coals

When Moses was still a baby growing up in the palace, Pharaoh's ministers were very jealous of him because Pharaoh loved him and paid so much attention to him. One day, the ministers saw baby Moses put Pharaoh's crown on his head. "Look!" they cried to Pharaoh. "Little Moses wants to take over the palace!" So they made a test for the baby. They placed two objects in front of Moses: a bright jewel and a burning piece of coal. They watched to see which of the objects Moses would pick up. If he reached for the jewel, they told Pharaoh, it would mean he was going to try to overthrow Pharaoh, and they would see that he was killed. If he picked up the coal, then his life would be spared. Naturally, like all babies, Moses reached toward the sparkling light of the jewel. But just as his little fingers were about to touch the jewel, an angel moved the baby's hand toward the coal. Quickly, Moses stuck his fingers into his mouth and burned his tongue. For the rest of his life, Moses stuttered when he talked, and his brother Aaron had to speak for him at important times.

3. How Did Moses Find Out That He Was Jewish?

When Moses was growing up in Pharaoh's palace, his sister Miriam often went to see him. She taught him about her people, their people, the Israelites. She sang him songs and told him stories about their slavery and hardship, and spoke to him of her dreams of freedom for them all.

4. Taking the First Step

When the Israelites left Egypt and came to the Reed Sea, Moses told them the sea would part. But no one wanted to go into the water. Everyone was afraid; no one moved. Then, suddenly, one brave man,

Nachshon ben Aminadav, took the first step. He stepped into the water until it reached his head. And then the sea parted so the Israelites could cross on dry land.

SEDER TALK

Taking Risks

The Book of Exodus in the Torah tells us: "And the Children of Israel went into the midst of the sea upon the dry ground." The ancient Rabbis talked about this, asking:

- If they went into the sea, then why does it say "upon dry ground"?
- And if they went "upon dry ground," then why does it say "in the midst of the sea"?

These are great questions! The ancient *midrash* says that the sea did not part to let the Israelites cross until they actually stepped into it, and until the water reached their noses! So maybe taking the risk is what parted the sea!

Maybe these Passover stories tell us that we all have to take risks sometimes to "get to the other side." Has there been a risk in your life that you were afraid to take, like diving off a diving board for the first time, moving to a new neighborhood, or changing schools? Did it seem quite so risky or scary once you came to the other side?

CUSTOM

Fruits from the Sea

The Book of Psalms tells us: "God led them through the depths. . . ." What does this mean? Rabbi Nehorai said: "While the Jews were leaving *Mitzrayim,* a woman was walking through the sea toward freedom, holding her small son by the hand. When the boy began to cry, she only had to reach out her hand and pick an apple or a pomegranate from the sea, and give it to him to comfort him."

Even today, Jewish people whose families came from Egypt put a bowl of pomegranate seeds on the seder table to remind them of the crossing of the Reed Sea. Cherie's friend, the Israeli poet Dr. Ada

Aharoni, who was born in Egypt, says that when she was a child, she always watched the bowl to see the water and the pomegranate seeds move.

To remember this *midrash*—a story written to explain what happened in the Bible—you can put a bowl of water and pomegranate seeds on your table.

Pomegranates grow in Israel. They are sweet and delicious, and they have many, many seeds. In fact, some people say that there are 613 seeds in a pomegranate, the same number as the 613 commandments in the Torah. Cherie likes to use the pomegranate on Passover to show that there are many, many good things in our lives, one good thing for each of the seeds!

FUN

Play a Game

This is a game that all of your seder guests can enjoy together. It's like a game you may remember from long ago: "I'm packing my grandmother's suitcase, and in the suitcase, I'm packing . . ."

Leah Glass, age 12

One person starts by saying, "I'm packing for the Exodus, and in my pack I'm taking . . . an apple!" (You can say anything that starts with the letter A.)

The next person has to say, "I'm packing for the Exodus, and in my pack I'm taking . . . an apple and . . . (something that starts with a B, like bitter herbs).

The next person has to say the first two, and then add a word that begins with C, like "clothes."

See if you can go all the way through the alphabet. Remember: you can take foods or Passover symbols or clothing or objects, but no *chametz,* no leavened foods!

THINK ABOUT HOW YOU CAN HELP THE
EARTH RENEW ITSELF IN THE SPRING.
CONSIDER WHAT YOU CAN DO TO HELP
MAKE SURE THAT THE EARTH KEEPS
GROWING, INSTEAD OF BEING DESTROYED.

15
The Exodus Story

Take a Nature Walk

So many flowers and plants reappear in the spring! Now that the days are warmer, you can spend the weeks before Passover walking outside to see nature's rebirth. (Go on your own or with friends or members of your family.) Stroll in the park, hike in the woods, visit the zoo, ride your bicycle into the hills to a nature preserve or to the botanical gardens. Or explore in your own backyard!

As you walk, look around—down at the new grass, up at the new leaves in the trees. What is in bloom? What has just been born? What is about to come back to life? What signs are still there from winter or from last summer?

After your adventure, you will be prepared to celebrate the holiday of renewal!

Plant a Parsley and Radish Garden

Long before Passover, you can start preparing for the holiday by planting parsley and radishes, which you can use on your seder plate. Some people plant parsley seeds at their *Tu B'Shevat* (**too b'shehv-AT**) seder (at the end of January or beginning of February) so that the parsley is ready in time for Passover. It's easy to plant parsley and radishes. Just fill a pot with good soil, put the seeds in the pot according to the directions on the package, and place the plants in a spot that will get plenty of sun. And don't forget to water the seeds!

Radish seeds take four to five days to sprout. Parsley needs two weeks to grow into bushy leaves. They both need two months to grow large enough to use at your seder. Best of all, you can plant extra seeds so that you'll have plants to give as Passover gifts to your guests and friends. You can decorate the outside of the pots with spring pictures from magazines. Just glue the pictures onto the pots, and spray the pictures with shellac.

Ishayah Waters, age 9

Create a Family Spring Poem

Create a spring poem with your family to help celebrate the season.

Everyone helps to create this poem. One person can start by saying something such as, "Spring is so beautiful!"

How beautiful is Spring
- in the morning light
- when the birds sing

Melody Mechanic, age 8

Then each person adds one line at a time to the poem, saying things like:

"Spring is so beautiful . . . with flowers blooming on trees."

"Spring is so beautiful . . . with baby birds chirping in nests."

"Spring is so beautiful . . . with bright sunshine on spider webs."

"Spring is so beautiful . . . in the morning light."

You can make your poem into a Passover poster. Simply draw the outline of a large flower on a big piece of paper, and then ask everyone to write a line for the poem on a computer label or strip of paper. Then paste them all on the flower. Presto! You have an instant spring poem picture to hang at your seder!

A SEDER READING

Many people in Israel live together in small communities, called *kibbutzim*. On many *kibbutzim* in Israel, the seder is begun with these words: "Here I am ready to perform the *mitzvah* (commandment) of observing spring and remembering the day when we went out of Egypt."

You may want to recite these words at your seder, too.

Zak Schwartz, age 17, and Cherie Karo Schwartz

MORE SEDER TALK

Blessing for the Land

Start a new tradition in your family. Offer a prayer for the earth:
"May the earth have a good, sweet, fruitful year!
May the earth be blessed with_____ and _____."
How will you fill in the blanks?

MORE FUN
An Extra-Hard Riddle

According to the classic *midrash,* this riddle was asked of King Solomon by the Queen of Sheba. He was so wise that he answered it! Can you figure it out?

Riddle: What land has seen the sun only once?

Clue: Think about the end of the Passover story!

Answer: The bottom of the Reed Sea, when it parted for the Israelites to cross, saw the sun for the one and only time!

Tsila Schwartz

A plague of lice (with Judeo-Arabic script).
Cairo Haggadah, Egypt, 1931

INTRODUCTION

Plagues come in many different forms. Thousands of years ago, God sent Moses and Aaron to warn Pharaoh about the plagues, which would descend upon the land. The plagues took the form of such things as blood and locusts, frogs, lice, and hail, and were seen as signs of God's power and might. They didn't go away until Pharaoh let the Jews leave Egypt.

Not all plagues are sent by God. Some are of our own making. In this chapter, you'll read more about the ten plagues of old and some new plagues, too.

STORY

We know from the Torah that at the time of the second plague the land of Egypt was covered with frogs. But the Torah doesn't use the Hebrew word for frogs; it uses the Hebrew word for only one frog. So how could *one* frog become many frogs?

The ancient Rabbis discussed this question and created a *midrash* to answer it. Rabbi Akiba, who lived in the first century, explained that there was only one frog, which gave birth to many frogs, which gave birth to many, many more frogs, until frogs were hopping everywhere!

Chapin Campbell, age 13

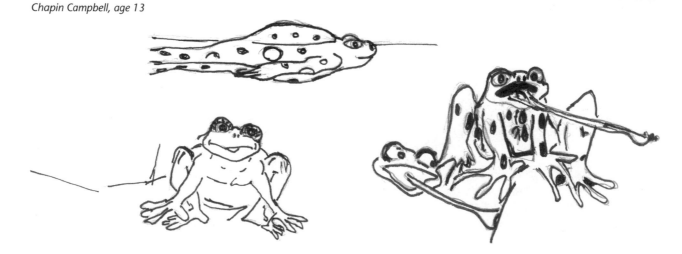

The Ten Plagues

But another Rabbi disagreed. "No way! That's not the way it was. First one frog came. That frog croaked for lots and lots of other frogs to come."

So, what do *you* think really happened? How did one frog become many, many frogs? (You can create your own story to answer the question!)

Today, many people write their own *midrashim* (plural of *midrash*) to explain the stories in the Bible. Here is Barbara's own explanation for how so many frogs came to land in Pharaoh's back yard:

Ethan Cohen, age 6

Frogs and More Frogs
by Barbara Rush

God sent a green frog hopping
right down to Egypt land.
He hopped and jumped and tumbled
across the desert sand.

And then he called his parents
and all his froggy kin
to hop to Pharaoh's palace
and let themselves right in.

Ethan Cohen, age 6

Into Pharaoh's pots and dishes,
and all that they could see,
those frogs just came a jumping
for one day, two, and three.

Right up to Pharaoh's shoulders
and in between his toes.
And then those silly froggies
just tickled Pharaoh's nose.

So many frogs were jumping,
they looked like froggy rain.
Those croaking, hopping creatures
were certainly a pain!

"Help! They're after me!"
Eisenstein Haggadah, U.S., 1928

Lucy Wohlauer, age 12

And then they spoke to Pharaoh:
"Please let those Hebrews go!"
And ticklish Pharaoh answered,
"All right, you froggy foe!"

The froggies stopped their tickling.
The Jews began to pack.
But then that wicked Pharaoh thought,
"Oh, my, I want them back!"

"I've changed my mind," thought Pharaoh.
"Indeed, what have I done?
Who will do the bitter work
when all the Jews are gone?"

So Pharaoh quickly shouted,
"No! No! No! No! No!
I'll never let it happen.
I won't let the Hebrews go!"

"Don't worry," God told Moses,
"I'll send a plague anew.
That wicked, wicked Pharaoh
will soon see what I can do."

And God did!
Question: What plague did God send next?

CRAFTS

A Froggy Critter

Cherie's Mom, Dotty Karo, makes froggy toys for decorating the seder table. You can toss them or play with them, too. Ask an adult to help you with this craft.

WHAT YOU NEED:

2 sheets of 8 ½" x 11" tracing paper
6–8 straight pins
large-eyed needle and heavy white thread
large, sharp scissors
green Naugahyde (14" x 8")

(list continued on p. 22)

Froggy Mouth (B)
RED

Fold in
(1 time)

FROGGY CRITTER

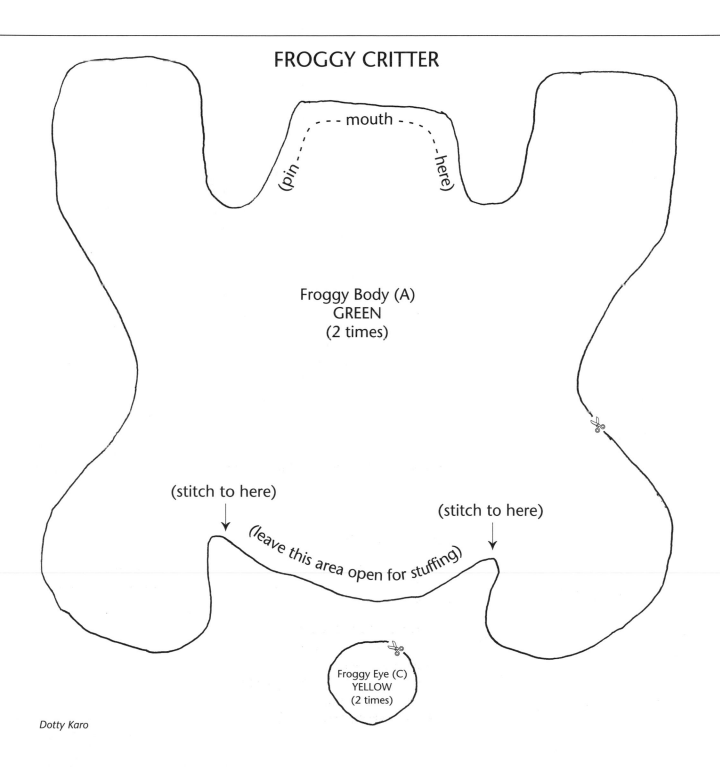

- - - mouth - - -

(pin   here)

Froggy Body (A)
GREEN
(2 times)

(stitch to here)

(stitch to here)

(leave this area open for stuffing)

Froggy Eye (C)
YELLOW
(2 times)

Dotty Karo

red Naugahyde (3" x 5")
yellow Naugahyde (2" x 2")
2–3 ounces of polyfill or cotton for stuffing
thimble for pushing needle through thick material

WHAT YOU DO:

1. Trace each of the froggy patterns (A, B, and C) shown here onto the pieces of paper and cut out the shapes to use as patterns.
2. Fold the green Naugahyde in half to form two 7" x 8" rectangles. Then pin the froggy body pattern (A) to the folded green Naugahyde. Carefully cut out two frog bodies. If it is too difficult to cut through the folded Naugahyde, then ask an adult to help you. Remove the pattern and pins.
3. Pin the froggy mouth pattern (B) to the red Naugahyde. Carefully cut out one froggy mouth. Remove the pattern and pins.
4. Fold the yellow Naugahyde in half to form a 1" x 2" rectangle. Then, pin the froggy eye pattern (C) to the folded yellow Naugahyde. Carefully cut out the two froggy eyes. Remove the pattern and pins.
5. Pin the eyes onto the top of one green body piece, and sew them on with an x-stitch (two stitches that cross each other to make the shape of an "x" in the middle of the frog's eye.) You can ask an adult to help you with this. Remove the pins after stitching.
6. Fold the red mouth in half, bright red side facing in.
7. Pin one half of the red mouth to the dull side of one of the green body pieces so that the mouth edges line up. Then pin the other half of the mouth onto the other green body piece so that the inside of the mouth is bright red as you look at the frog.
8. With whipstitches, sew across only the mouth area on both sides. (If you do not know what a whipstitch is, ask an adult to show you.) Remove the pins from the mouth.
9. Pin the two green body pieces together, bright green side out.
10. With whipstitches, sew the two body pieces together, beginning at the edge of the mouth, around the top leg, down the side, and around the back leg. Leave the bottom open for stuffing.
11. Make a double knot to hold the stitches in place and cut the thread.
12. Start again on the other side of the mouth, and repeat steps 9 and 10. Remove the pins.
13. Stuff the frog with the polyfill or cotton. Be sure to fill the feet!
14. Sew the bottom together with whipstitches. You now have a froggy critter!

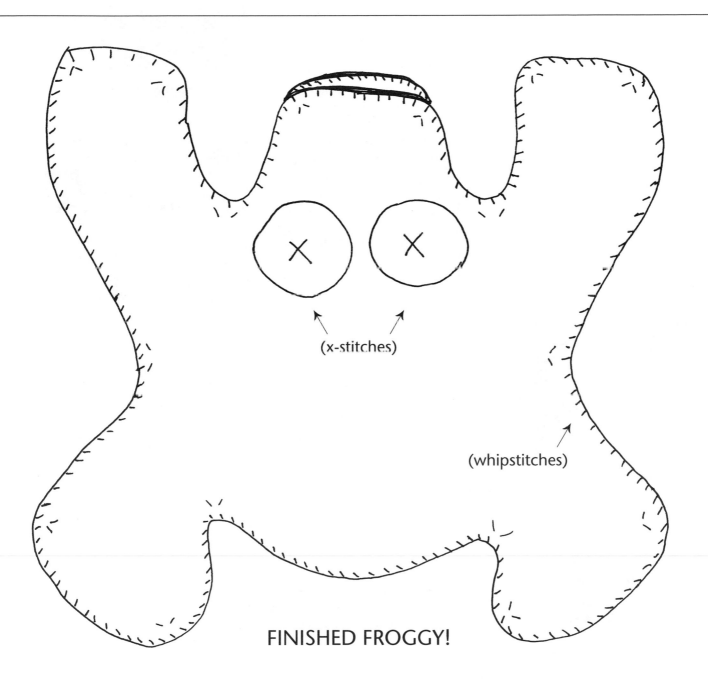

(x-stitches)

(whipstitches)

FINISHED FROGGY!

A Plague of Puppets

What if the Ten Plagues could talk? What would they say? Here's a chance to make simple puppets out of paper lunch bags, using magic markers or crayons, to create your own puppet play.

Shoshanah Grace, age 7

WHAT YOU NEED:

5" x 11" paper bag for each puppet
magic markers or crayons in different colors

WHAT YOU DO:

1. Lay the bag flat on a table with the side with the flap facing toward you (face up).
2. Draw on each puppet to make it look like one of the plagues: blood, frogs, lice, wild beasts, pestilence, boils, hail, locusts, darkness, or the slaying of the firstborn.
3. Draw half a mouth (the top lip) on the top of the flap, the other half (the lower lip) on the bag just below the bottom of the flap, so the mouth can move when the puppet talks.

Let each seder guest play with one or two of the puppets. After each puppet introduces itself to the seder guests, the puppets can talk to each other. Here is a sample script:

PUPPET 1: Hi! I'm a frog who lives in the land of Egypt. I'm having an incredible time jumping and hopping around everywhere. This morning I jumped right into Pharaoh's bed and tickled him awake! He didn't like that very much, but I sure did! No one knows what to do about us frogs! Wow! We frogs are really powerful! And every drop of water in Egypt is turning into one of my relatives. We are everywhere!

PUPPET 2: So you think that you're so great? I'm hail. I'm one of millions and billions and zillions of hail balls falling from the sky all

"Do you recognize me? I'm lice!"

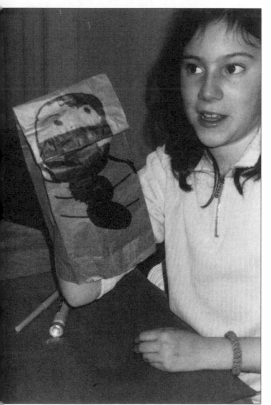

over Egypt. We're cold, we're hard, and we're right on target! There's hail in the houses, hail in the fields, and hail right on Pharaoh's crown! Now, see? That's power!

PUPPET 3: You think so? What can you see when I'm around? Nothing! I'm darkness, darker than the darkest night! People can't see where they're going. They're afraid of getting lost and bumping into things. That's real power!

Keep going until all the plagues have spoken, or create a different script.

FUN

Scrambled Plagues

The plagues really scrambled the life of Pharaoh! He never figured them out until the tenth plague. So, here's a great word scramble of the Ten Plagues. Can you figure them out?

LSIOB   SOCLUT   SCEITLPNE   GROSF   SKNDSAER

ELIC   ATSSBE   ALIH   YLGNAIS   DOOLB

After you unscramble these plagues, put them into their right order:

Geismar Haggadah, Germany, 1928

_____

_____

_____

_____

_____

_____

_____

_____

An Interview with Pharaoh

Pharaoh made the lives of the Jews very harsh. Did you ever wonder what he was thinking? Appoint someone at your seder table—someone who knows a lot about the Passover story—to play the role of Pharaoh. You and the other guests can ask him questions. You might even make a crown of cardboard or paper for "Pharaoh" to wear and use a microphone and tape recorder to interview him!

Here are some questions you might ask:

Why don't you want to let the Hebrew people go?

Why don't you let other people do all the hard work for a change?

What do you think will happen if you don't listen to Moses and Aaron?

Make your questions tricky and interesting!

CUSTOMS

Ten Drops of Wine

During the seder, when reciting each of the Ten Plagues, many Jews dip their smallest finger (or a spoon) into their wine glasses at the mention of each plague, then shake a drop of wine onto a small plate to symbolize each plague.

Why do we dip our finger into the wine?

The Bible tells us that by God's "hand" many great wonders were done, and with God's "finger" the plagues were sent upon Pharaoh. To remember God's act in our liberation, we dip our finger into the wine.

Judy Lande Haran

Bowl of Wine (from Morocco)

Some Jews from Morocco don't spill the wine onto their plates. Instead, they follow a very different custom. The mother holds a bowl of water and the father holds a bowl of wine. As each plague is named, they pour a bit of wine and water into a third bowl. Then the bowl of mixed water and wine is passed over the head of each unmarried person at the *seder.* Why? Some Moroccan Jews believe it can bring good luck or protection, just as the blood on the doorposts of the houses in Egypt protected the Children of Israel from the tenth plague.

But that's only one explanation. Others say that wine is a symbol of joy. When we fill our wine cups, we remember our happiness in leaving Egypt. But we should also remember the Egyptian soldiers who were drowned. Even though they were our enemies, they were also God's children. So some people suggest we should not be completely happy at this moment. We should not drink with a full cup. Instead, we remove a drop of wine as we recite each plague.

You may wonder what we do with the wine once it is spilled.

Many Jews spill out the wine and throw it away. Some even throw the wine glasses away, too!

SEDER TALK
What Are Some New Plagues in Our World?

There are some plagues that we can *see:* trash in the streets, forests cut down, polluted water . . .
And there are some plagues that we can *feel:* prejudice, bad attitude, jealousy . . .
Can you think of others?

How can *you* help get rid of the plagues in our lives?

INTRODUCTION

Question: Who are—and are not—at the Passover seder?

Answer: The women! If you've read the Haggadah, *you've already discovered that the brave women who hid children from Pharaoh's soldiers; Yocheved, who gave birth to Moses; and Miriam, who helped rescue her baby brother, are not mentioned in its pages. The Talmud (in Sotah) tells us that it was because of the deeds of the Hebrew women that the Jews were brought out of slavery in* Mitzrayim. *Yet these Hebrew women are not mentioned in the* Haggadah. *Even so, we feel their presence at the seder, and we remember them, as we also remember Puah and Shifrah, the brave midwives who saved Hebrew babies, and the daughter of Pharaoh who saved baby Moses. In this chapter, you'll find out more about these women and how to honor them—not just at your* seder *table, but in your daily life, as well.*

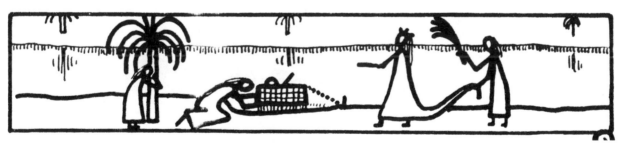

Can you find: Pharaoh's daughter, her servant, Baby Moses, Miriam, and Yocheved? (Clue: Someone's mother is hiding behind the tree.)
Geismar Haggadah, Germany, 1928

STORY

The Torah mentions Miriam's tambourine in Exodus 15:20. It says that Miriam took a timbrel (a musical instrument like a tambourine) in her hand and danced with the women at the shore of the sea they had just crossed. From ancient to modern times, people have created stories about Miriam. This is Cherie's modern *midrash* about Miriam's tambourine.

Miriam and the Women 3

Miriam and Her Tambourine
by Cherie Karo Schwartz

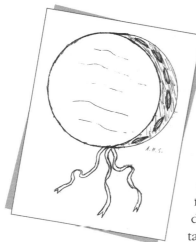

Aaron Schwartz, age 14

I am Miriam: woman of dreams, of song, and of the well. I am Miriam, sister of Moses, and I am Miriam of the tambourine. For all of my life, I have sung: to the babies I helped bring to life, to the Nile River, which saved my brother Moses, to the rock that brought forth water for us to drink . . . And I have sung with my tambourine.

When we, all of the Children of Israel, left our slavery in Egypt, we were in such a hurry, but I stopped long enough to pick up my tambourine. It had always been my companion, and I took it with me into the land of freedom.

Now we have crossed the Reed Sea out of Egypt and we are on the other side. Everyone and everything is in complete confusion. But I know what to do: I pick up my tambourine and slowly begin to sing and dance to the music. When the other women see me, they, too, begin to sing and sway. The sound of the tambourine helps us to remember our safe escape and to be thankful.

I place my tambourine carefully into my pack, and we begin our march to freedom. Sometimes the endless walking in the desert and the hot sun are so harsh, but then I hear the sound of the bells of my tambourine. Its music gives me new strength to go on.

At night I take out my tambourine and sing to the people, my people. The tambourine and our songs remind us of our sweet traditions, and its bells are bells of freedom.

We wander for forty years, and every day we hear the sound of my tambourine, giving us courage and hope. Each day we grow closer to our new home.

Now I am old. I am tired. I know that I will not live to see the end

Zak Schwartz, age 17

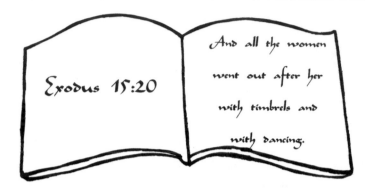

Exodus 15:20

And all the women went out after her with timbrels and with dancing.

of our journey. My resting place will be here, in the desert, on our way.

But what will happen to my tambourine? Well, I will tell you this much. I have seen it in a dream. Just before my soul is to be taken, the women come to me and play upon their own timbrels. The sound, like a heartbeat of life, gives me great comfort. I ask the women to help me to the well. I look into its deep and pure waters, and I see our future in the Promised Land.

This pleases me, but am I to take my tambourine to the grave with me? Ah, no. With my last ounce of strength, I throw my precious tambourine into the well and watch it slowly sink without a sound into the cool waters. Goodbye my friend, my freedom friend. We have found our freedom.

It is said that after I died, my well, Miriam's Well, stopped flowing and there was no more water, that the well just disappeared. So what became of the well and of my tambourine? It is still singing its songs of freedom. If you ever come across a well in the desert places, or anywhere in our sacred land of Israel, stop for a moment and really listen. You will be able to hear a sound coming from deep beneath the earth, the sound of a drum with little bells, the sound of freedom coming from my tambourine. It is a sound to remember.

FUN
Create a Story

Create your own story or *midrash* about something besides a tambourine that Miriam may have taken with her on her journey.

Miriam took something special with her, something that meant a lot to her and which she knew would be useful in a new land. It was not something for survival (like food); it was music to help sustain her spirit. The music reminded her of freedom.

If you had been with the Israelites as they were leaving the land of slavery, what very special thing would you have taken with you? Make this special thing, or draw a picture of it to go with your story.

Larry Schwartz

CRAFT

Miriam's Tambourine

WHAT YOU NEED:

2 lightweight 9-inch plastic picnic plates
6 pieces of colored yarn (any color), each 4 inches
　　long
6 jingle bells
hole punch
water color or "school" paints
a small paint brush
cellophane tape

WHAT YOU DO:

1. Place the two plates together so that their rims meet and there is a hollow space inside. Lightly tape the edges together.
2. Carefully punch holes into the plates at six evenly-spaced places around the rims.
3. String a piece of yarn through the loop on one of the bells. Do the same with the remaining pieces of yarn and the remaining bells.
4. Tie one string with a bell to each of the six holes around the edge of the plates. Tie each one with three knots. This will hold the two plates together. Then, remove the tape.
5. If you wish, paint designs or words or pictures on the outside of your tambourine.

SONG

Sing "Miriam's Slow Snake Dance" as you dance around your seder table while playing your tambourines, drums, or other instruments, or "dance" with your hands at the table. Invite everyone to play and sway to the music.

Turn the page for the music

Miriam's Slow Snake Dance by the Riverside

A round in three parts
Linda Hirschhorn

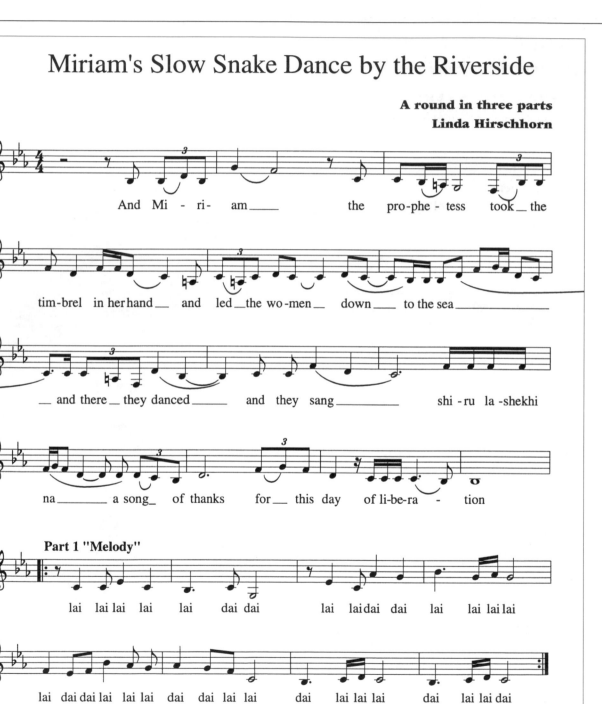

Part 2 "The Call"

Miriam, come quickly and teach us your dances!

Turn the page for Part 3

Part 3 "The Celebration"

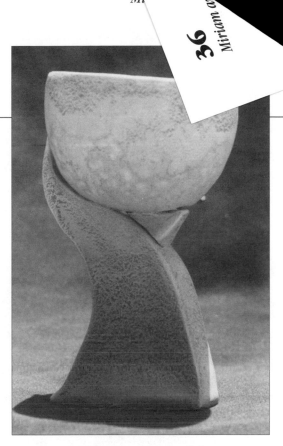

A Miriam's cup made of clay.
Joan Cohen

CUSTOM

A Cup for Miriam

Some people set a special cup (in Hebrew, *kos Miryam*) on the seder table in honor of Miriam and as a reminder of Miriam's Well of sweet, healing, and refreshing water, which followed the Israelites in the desert.

Miriam's Cup can be filled with plain water or spring water. Sometimes it is left empty, and everyone at the seder table pours a bit of water from his or her own glass into Miriam's Cup until it's filled. In this way, everyone participates in creating the *Ma'ayan,* the wellspring of Miriam's Well.

Of course, there are different traditions for Miriam's Cup. Some people fill the cup with wine. Others paint the cup blue as a reminder of the water in Miriam's Well. Some people even dangle shells or bells from the cup to remember the sound of Miriam's tambourine.

Miriam's Cup.
Lucy Schwartz, age 15

MORE FUN

A Bowl for Miriam

According to tradition, during the forty years of wandering in the desert, Miriam's Well provided the Jews with water. It is said that herbs and plants grew around the well, and that the well was filled with sweet-smelling spices. Everyone who tasted the water felt refreshed. As a reminder of Miriam's Well, you may want to make a sweet-smelling bowl to place on your seder table.

1. Fill a clear glass bowl with water (or use rosewater).
2. Add cinnamon and cloves. (It is said that these are the spices that Adam and Eve took with them as they left the Garden of Eden. That's why they are used for the *besamim,* the spices at *Havdalah,* at the end of Shabbat.)
3. Float rose petals or other flower petals on the water to make it more beautiful and fragrant.

SEDER READINGS

Remembering the Women

You may want to read this at your seder:

Passover is a time to remember that we are descendants of the brave women from the Passover story: Yocheved, who gave birth to Moses; Miriam, who led her people to freedom; and all the Hebrew mothers who worked hard in Egypt taking care of their families. The Talmud (in *Sotah*) tells us that because of their labors, the Children of Israel were set free.

If you like, you may also read aloud Cherie's poem-song at your seder and clap or drum along to the rythm:

How the Women Came Dancing

> Here is a story—
> a story of brave women,
> a story of how the women
> came dancing to freedom
> as we left *Mitzrayim* long ago.

Miriam and the women dancing.
Geismar Haggadah, Germany, 1928

> Here is a story—
> a story of Yocheved,
> birthing Aaron, birthing Miriam,
> birthing the baby Moses
> in *Mitzrayim* long ago.

> Here is a story—
> a story of Miriam
> dreaming of Moses,
> sharing stories of his people,
> drumming her tambourine,
> in *Mitzrayim* long ago.

Here is a story—
a story of Shifrah and Puah,
brave midwives defying Pharaoh,
saving Jewish baby boys
in *Mitzrayim* long ago.

Here is a story—
a story of Pharaoh's daughter,
finding Moses in a reed basket,
and raising him in the palace
in *Mitzrayim* long ago.

Here is a story—
a story of the women
crossing the sea to freedom,
dancing with their timbrels
in the desert long ago.

Here is our story—
a story of women's courage,
praying, singing, crying, weeping,
as they helped us leave *Mitzrayim,*
dancing to freedom long ago.

Judy Lande Haran

This poem honors the women who played an important role in the story of Passover. There are many other courageous women in Jewish history. Do you know about the Matriarchs (**MAY-tree-arks**): Sarah, Rebecca, Rachel, and Leah? What about Queen Esther, Hannah Senesch, or Golda Meir? Who are some famous Jewish women today? Who are some of the women who are important in your own life?

How do women today continue to help the Jewish people remain free? Can you and your seder guests create a blessing to celebrate the women?

SEDER TALK
A Difficult Question about the Midwives

The midwives, Shifrah and Puah, disobeyed Pharaoh. He told them to kill the Hebrew babies, but they refused. Should they have disobeyed the law?

Are some laws or rules unfair? Should you follow the rules, even if they are unjust? Or should you disobey them? What do you think?

INTRODUCTION

The story of the Exodus is the story of the Jewish people's journey to freedom. But what does freedom mean? How can we celebrate freedom each year as if we ourselves were freed from Egypt?

In this chapter you'll discover new ways to think about freedom. Does freedom mean something different today than it did years ago? Will it mean something different for future generations? How can we understand freedom as Jews, as individuals, and as people of the world?

Lucy Schwartz, age 15

STORY

This story was written by eleven-year-old Rachel Petroff. Her mother, Cherie's friend, had asked her a question, "What do you think it would have been like to leave Egypt with Moses?" Rachel responded by creating this story!

Lauren Jennifer Staub, age 12

The Children Are the Future

by Rachel Sara Petroff, age 11

"Let's go! Let's go. Move it! Move it! Faster, *faster*! Men, bring up the rear! Everyone get with your tribe! No! No! Your tribe over here and your tribe over there! Tribe of Judah! Move it!"

The field, filled with men and women running in every direction, was not a pretty sight. "You know what, Sara?" I asked my best friend whose family was sharing a cart with us.

"What?" she asked.

"These people are crazy. I just know it. I mean this old guy comes in, says God will save us, and everyone starts going crazy! Personally, I'm glad to be leaving Egypt, but I think we're cursed! Think about it, all these spooky things happened as soon as our parents told us that we shall be redeemed!"

At that moment a loud ram's horn sounded through the field. Everyone scrambled toward the wagons. The line of horses and donkeys began moving. This was it! I was excited

deep down, but still afraid God would send more plagues before we were safely away.

"Okay, honey, this is it!" My mother called to me over her shoulder as we moved forward with the crowd of children and mothers, slowly and loudly surging toward the desert and the sea. "The event you'll remember for a lifetime."

I was having great fun, calling out to my friends from the back of the cart and watching all the animals. I love horses and donkeys. Honest, I do!

Then it happened. From the back of the crowd came a cry.

"The Egyptians are coming! The chariots are coming!"

The cry made everyone panic. Babies began to cry. Fathers whipped the donkeys. Mothers held their children tightly. Then we reached the Red Sea! It was either sink (and die) or swim.

"Sara," I whispered so my parents wouldn't hear me, "come on!"

"Where are we going?"

"Shush! Not so loud! Follow me."

In all the commotion, no one noticed two young girls creeping away from our cart and running to the edge of the sea.

"Well, where are we going?"

"The Egyptians are coming," I said. "They have the biggest army around. They'll kill the old and young and take the rest back to Egypt. We can't stay here!"

"You mean we're going to swim?"

"That's exactly what I mean."

"Rachel, we'll get killed!"

"But we'd get killed anyway. This way, if we die, we die trying to live."

I looked out at the dark water and gasped. The Red Sea was large. Very large.

Then I saw Moses. He was kneeling at the edge of the Red Sea. I guess he was praying to God.

"Moses!" I cried. "Get up off your knees and save us! You want us all to get killed?!?!"

Lauren Jennifer Staub, age 12

"Children, children, what are you doing here?"

"The Egyptians are coming! We're trying to get across the Red Sea so they won't kill us."

"Girls, what are your names?"

"Sara."

"Rachel," I said.

"Sara, Rachel, I need your help. God asked me to split the sea, but says I need help from the future. You are the closest to a promising future I've seen all day."

"What do we have to do?" Sara asked.

"Sara, you hold the staff. Rachel, I need you to go to the wagons and arrange them in lines. Take this with you." To my surprise, I was handed a whistle made of wood.

Dutifully, I went along. How would I get this mass of people into lines? I blew the whistle sharply. "Let's go!" I shouted. "Hurry! Boys under thirteen in the first six carts. Girls under thirteen in the second six carts! Hurry! Each tribe form a line. Let's have some order now! Move!"

"Please, God, " I said under my breath, "make this work."

I waited for utter chaos to break out. It didn't. No one had heard

Dressing Our Dolls for Their Journey to Freedom

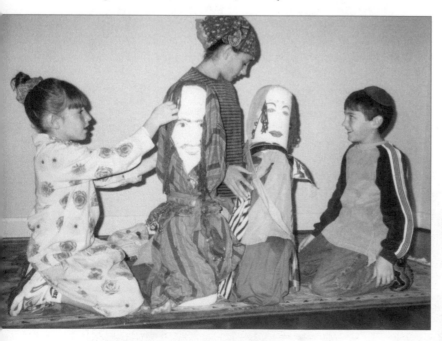

me. People were too loud. Slowly I blew the whistle again, expecting a loud piercing sound, but there wasn't one. Instead, I didn't hear anything. I sighed and looked at the ground. Suddenly it was very quiet. I looked up to see everyone in a straight line! All the children were in the carts exactly where they should have been. I was astonished. Utterly astonished.

Following Moses' instruction, I went back to the edge of the sea. Sara was holding the staff, and Moses cried out:

"Split the sea for our children! Open it for our future!"

To my utter astonishment, the sea walls reared back.

"Girls," Moses yelled to Sara and me, "run. Run to your place in line. Hurry!"

After we had made it through the sea, and the danger had passed, Moses took me aside and told me the magic of the whistle.

"It isn't magic, really. It can make a prayer come true to a worthy caretaker of the Jewish people. If you weren't worthy of carrying on the traditions of the Jewish people, it wouldn't have worked. But you *are* worthy. We have children worthy of our future. And that is the biggest miracle of all."

Aaron Schwartz, age 14

CRAFT

A Freedom Banner

Long ago Jews used to make banners for special holidays. Since Passover is a holiday celebrating freedom, you can make a "freedom banner" to hang near your seder table. Decorate your banner to show how you feel about freedom in your life. Place a beautiful border around your banner to show the beauty of freedom.

WHAT YOU NEED:

paper, craft felt, or fabric (11" x 14" is a good size, but your banner can be any size or shape)
a sheet of paper (smaller than the paper, felt, or fabric, but big enough to fit a poem, blessing, or short story)
pencil
pens, magic markers, or paints
a 12"-long wooden dowel that is 1/2" in diameter
18" of any color yarn
a small picture hanger
rubber cement

WHAT YOU DO:

1. Before you make the banner, you need to create the words to go on it. Here are some ideas: Write a poem about how people should live in freedom; create a blessing or prayer asking God for freedom everywhere; or tell a short story about how someone found personal or political freedom.

2. Write your short story, blessing, or poem on the sheet of paper, then glue or tape it to the center of the paper, felt, or fabric you are using for your banner.

3. Create a border for your banner by drawing different designs in pencil around your short story, poem, or blessing. You could create circles, squares, and ovals, all touching each other. Or you could create pictures of the sky, with clouds, stars, the sun, or birds flying free. You may want to draw hands of many colors, touching each other around the edge of the border.

4. When you are done drawing your border design, color it with pens, magic markers, or paints.

5. Lay the finished banner flat on a table. Apply rubber cement across the top edge of the banner. Lay the dowel along the cemented edge and roll the top of the banner over the dowel to cover the dowel. You may need to apply a bit more rubber cement as you roll. After you finish rolling, place a heavy book or two over the covered dowel to secure the banner until the cement dries.

6. When the banner is dry, attach the yarn to it. Tie the ends of the yarn onto either end of the dowel. Secure the yarn with double knots.

7. Put up the small picture hanger on the wall. Hang your banner on the hanger by the yarn loop.

SONGS

Hymn of the Partisans

During the Holocaust, the Jews created many songs to help keep up their hope and faith. Jews in the concentration camps of World War II sang this song. The words show that, even during the darkest days, there was still hope for freedom. We can still sing these words today:

Never say that you are going the last way
Though leaden skies hide the bright blue light of day.
The freedom that we longed for will appear.
It will drum our marching steps, for we are here!

זאָג ניט קיינמאָל אַז דו גייסט דעם לעצטן וועג,
ווען הימלען בלייענע פאַרשטעלן בלויע טעג.
ווייל קומען וועט נאָך אונדזער אויסגעבענקטע שעה,
ס׳וועט אַ פויק טאָן אונדזער טראָט: מיר זיינען דאָ!

פון גרינעם פּאַלמען-לאַנד ביז ווייסן לאַנד פון שניי,
מיר זיינען דאָ, מיט אונדזער פּיין, מיט אונדזער וויי.
און ווו געפאַלן ס׳איז אַ שפּריץ פון אונדזער בלוט,
וועט אַ שפּראָץ טאָן אונדזער גבורה, אונדזער מוט.

The Yiddish lyrics to the "Hymn of the Partisans."

This song, from "Hymn of the Partisans," was written by Hirsh Glick. It was translated from the Yiddish by Barbara Rush.

Wandering

Words & Music
Fran Avni

When will all this wan-d'ring e-ver cease_____

when will we set-tle down and live in peace?_____ We're

tired of wan-d'ring through the wil-der-ness_____ It's

time for all our peo-ple now to rest_____

Refrain

Lord it is-n't ea-sy Lord it is-n't ea-sy

Lords it is-n't ea-sy to be free_____

When will we ever reach the Promised Land?
All our eyes can see are hills of sand
We finally got away from slavery
But Lord it isn't easy to be free
Refrain
O Lord it isn't easy (3x) to be free

Though years go by and we're still on our way
Our hopes and dreams get stronger every day
We know that we were led out of slavery
So all our children's children could be free
Refrain

Many people sing this traditional Passover song at the seder. It tells of our slavery in ancient times.

We were slaves to Pharoah in Egypt
We were slaves, and now we are free!

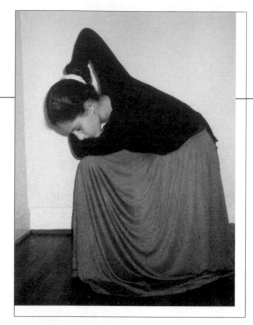

"Once we were slaves."

"Now we're free!"

SEDER TALK

What Does It Mean To Be Free?

What does it mean to be free? Should we have the freedom to do whatever we want? What are the limits? May you do whatever you feel like doing, even if it could hurt someone or hurt someone's feelings? What if you do something that makes *you* feel free, but it could take away someone else's freedom? And once we have become free, what responsibilities do we have to others who are also free? What about our responsibilities to those who are not yet free?

Our Jewish tradition tells us that all people are responsible for each other, and that no one is truly free until everyone is free. What do you think about this?

Freedom Wishes

Freedom works two ways. What does this mean? There are some things that we want freedom to *do,* like to be with our friends. And, there are some things that we want freedom *from,* like prejudice and hatred. People at your seder table can talk about these different kinds of freedom and make their own "freedom" promises, such as:

"This year I will try to bring freedom to _____."

"This year I will try to gain freedom from _____."

CUSTOM

"B'ivhilut" (from Morocco)

Barbara's friend, Simha Shemesh, was born in Morocco, where some Moroccan Jews sing a special song called *"B'ivhilut"* during the seder. The words mean "In haste we left Egypt. This is the bread of affliction. We were slaves. Now we are free."

As everyone sings the song, the mother lifts the seder plate and guides it over the heads of everyone at the table—and of everyone in the house, even over the heads of the babies in other

rooms who may be sleeping! This custom in Simha's family still helps to make sure that everyone in the house continues to be free. (If the seder plate is too heavy, then the mother can use a plate filled with beautiful flowers instead!)

MORE SEDER TALK

ASL—Another Way to Say "Freedom"

Many people who cannot hear use their own language of signing. One type of signing is called American Sign Language (ASL). Here is the sign for "Freedom" in ASL:

Judy Lande Haran

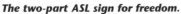

The two-part ASL sign for freedom.

Showing That We Are Free

Question: What are some ways at the seder that we show that we are free?

Answers:

1. Slaves in ancient Egypt had to stand while they ate. The Jews sit reclining with pillows at their seats to show that they are free.
2. Some Jews wear white clothing at the seder because white is a color of freedom.
3. The Jews eat *matzah*, special flat bread, at Passover, as a reminder of the bread the Israelites ate on their way to freedom.
4. We sing about our freedom.

A SEDER READING

Freedom is an important idea to remember during Passover and all year long. You may want to read this at your seder.

We Were Slaves

Every year, we are reminded that we were slaves in *Mitzrayim*. We were mistreated, oppressed, enslaved, and not respected. We were not allowed to be free. So we must remember always to treat other people with respect and honor.

PROJECT

A Seder for Everyone

What can *you* do to help others celebrate freedom? It is our tradition to help every Jew, no matter how poor, to have a seder. Are there people in your community who cannot afford to make a seder? Here are some ideas about how you can help:

Can you and your friends do some special chores or projects to earn some extra money, and then donate this money to help make seders in a shelter, hospital, or home for senior citizens?

Can you and your family or club volunteer to help large families or elderly families clean their houses to help get ready for Passover?

Geismar Haggadah, Germany, 1928

"We are celebrating freedom."

Judy Lande Haran

Preparing for the Seder

*I*t's spring! This is a very special time of the year for Jews because only one month remains after the fun-filled holiday of *Purim* to prepare for Passover.

There is so much to do: guests to invite, *matzah* and horseradish to buy (or make), and the seder plate—with the *karpas,* bone, eggs, *maror,* and *charoset*—to prepare. The *Haggadot* from last year must be hauled down from the attic or uncovered in the hall closet, one copy for each guest. And every room of the house, every corner of the apartment, must be cleaned from top to bottom. By the time Passover begins, no *chametz* should be found anywhere. In this section you will learn about the different ways that Jews around the world prepare for Passover.

INTRODUCTION

Passover is a time when we eat so many special foods. Most Jews today buy matzot *and Passover foods in the supermarket. It's expensive to prepare a seder, but most Jews earn enough money to celebrate the holiday properly. But it was not always so easy to prepare for Passover. In many countries Jews couldn't afford the special foods needed for the seder. Read this story to find out how one family solved this problem.*

STORY

A Letter to God

A folktale from Iran, retold by Barbara Rush

Shumel (**SHOO-mell**), the clothes presser, put down his heavy iron and sighed in despair. A serious problem kept him from concentrating on his work. The holiday of *Pesach* was coming, and there was not enough money to make a seder for his family.

Life was hard in the small Persian village where he lived with his wife, Chabas, and their ten little ones. All the sunlit hours of the day Shumel lifted the iron and pressed, piece after piece, the clothes that the Jews of the town brought to him. Who could count the hours after dark when he sat, under a dimly lit lamp, pressing quickly to finish a job? And yet Shumel did not complain.

But now that the days of *Pesach* were approaching, he was quite disheartened. "Ah," Shumel thought to himself, "how can we have the holiday without a seder? What will *Pesach* be like without *matzot* and wine to put on the table?"

Shumel pressed another sleeve of a shirt and again paused to think. "All year long I have not been able to save an extra coin for the holiday. And now, who will help me? There is no one from whom I can borrow the money."

All afternoon Shumel sat, pressing and thinking. "Alas," he said aloud. "I will write a letter to God. Yes, I will ask God for the money."

That evening, after Shumel finished his day's ironing and ate his evening meal, he took out a piece of fresh paper, lit the lamp, and prepared to write. Now, Shumel was a man of little education and was not

"We're cleaning for Passover!"

accustomed to writing letters of such importance. After all, how often was it that one wrote a letter to God? For a long while he sat and thought. Finally, with a trembling hand, he wrote his simple request.

After Shumel reread the letter and was satisfied with its contents, he sealed it and went to bed, hopeful that God would answer his plea. In the morning, before he started his ironing, he took the letter to the post office and went off to his day's work.

Brian Raphael, age 16

The clerk in the post office read the address on Shumel's letter and was quite perplexed. "A letter to God?" he thought to himself. "Where shall I send it?"

The letter was shifted from one clerk to another. Each clerk was equally puzzled by the strange address. At last the letter reached the desk of Mohammed Ussif, the postmaster, who opened the envelope and read aloud:

> "Dear God,
> The holiday of *Pesach* is coming, and I do not have enough money to make a seder for my family. You must know, God, how hard I have worked pressing clothes this past year, but I have not been able to save an extra coin for the holiday. Believe me, God, I am embarrassed to ask you for favors, but there is no one else I can turn to for help. I have ten children. For their sakes I am begging you to send ten *lirot,* ten coins.
> Thank you, God.
>
> (signed) Shumel"

Now, Mohammed Ussif was a man not usually known for his compassion. But as he read the letter, the room became silent. Even he was touched by the plight of the poor Jew.

"Take pity on this man!" Mohammed said quickly, as if afraid that he would soon change his mind. "Each of us must dig into his pocket and find a coin for this poor family."

Mohammed and each of his clerks reached into a pocket and pulled out a coin. Together nine *lirot* were counted, and sent in an envelope to the poor Jew.

Can you imagine Shumel's excitement when he saw the money?

Matzot and wine were bought for the seder. Chabas was radiant in her new dress. Shumel sat happily at the table, beaming on his family with feelings of thanks and joy.

Another year passed. Shumel worked hard, day after day, from morning to night, lifting the iron, pressing the clothes. But, again the holiday of *Pesach* approached, and again he did not have enough money to buy wine, *matzot,* or other holiday food. What could the poor man do? Once again he decided to write a letter to God.

And so Shumel sat down, took out a clean piece of paper, pen and ink, and wrote:

> "Dear God,
> Thank you for the money you sent us last year for *Pesach*. My wife Chabas bought a new dress, and we all had wine and *matzot* and good food for the seder.
>
> You must know that I have worked hard all year long, but now that the holiday of *Pesach* is coming again, I do not have enough money to make a seder for my family. If you remember, God, I have ten children. Please send us ten *lirot,* and we will be able to celebrate properly."

Shumel was about to sign the letter, but then he paused, thought quickly, and added a few lines:

> "Dear God, I am ashamed to tell you that last year when you sent the money through the post office, there were thieves there who kept one *lira* for themselves. So this year I would like to ask a favor of you. Please, dear God, if it's not too much trouble, send the money directly to me."

BEFORE-SEDER TALK
Who Will Come to Your Seder?

You can help make sure that everyone has the chance to participate in a seder. Many people invite family, friends, and neighbors, as well as someone new in town, such as students at a local college, or someone passing through town who might not otherwise have a seder.

It is also a tradition to invite someone who is not Jewish to the seder. By explaining the Passover customs and story to your guest, your family can learn new things about the holiday and enjoy and understand Passover—and the meaning of freedom—even more. Also, by inviting someone who isn't Jewish to your seder you have the opportunity to help different peoples understand each other better.

CRAFT

A Seder Invitation

Noah Hertz Marks, age 7

Many people invite guests to their seders. It is a special blessing to have guests, especially on Passover, when we are told in the *Haggadah* to "Let all who are hungry come and eat!"

In Cherie's family, there are always surprise guests, bringing with them riches from other cultures—African American, Chinese, Scottish, Mexican, Irish, Japanese, Native American, Iranian. These guests make the celebration of freedom even more special! Often, seder invitations are given over the phone, but you can create your own beautiful seder invitation to send in the mail!

WHAT YOU NEED:

heavy-weight white typewriter paper, 8½" x 11"

pencil

ruler

Post-It correction and cover-up tape, 1/3" wide (you can buy it at an office supply store)

scissors

eraser

magic markers in a variety of colors

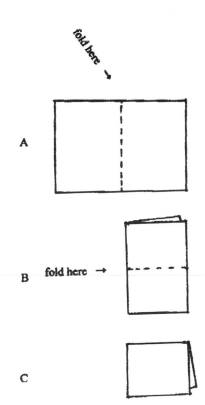

Don Rush

WHAT YOU DO:

1. Fold the paper in half vertically, and in half again horizontally, so that it measures 5 1/2" x 4".

2. Put it down in front of you so that the unfolded edges are at the bottom. Using the ruler, make two horizontal guidelines on the front of the card. They should be about two inches apart. The lines will help keep the letters uniform.

3. Cut strips of the white tape to form the letters of the word "*matzah*" (in Hebrew מצה) on the card. You may want to write the Hebrew word for *Pesach* or seder instead. Stay between the

Noah Hertz Marks, age 7

two horizontal lines. Each letter will take up approximately one to two inches across. The מ will need more room than the other letters. (Notice that you will need four separate pieces of tape for the letter מ; three pieces for the letter צ; and three pieces for the ה.) Be sure to overlap the pieces of tape as you construct each letter. Don't worry if this looks messy because you will soon discard the tape.

4. When the word *matzah* is formed, erase the two horizontal lines you drew in earlier with your pencil.
5. Using different colored magic markers, trace around each letter. Be sure to touch all the edges.
6. When the magic marker is completely dry, remove the tape.
7. Write your invitation on the inside of the card.
8. For more invitations, make each card individually or duplicate the card on a copying machine. Open the page to its fullest size, and both the front picture and the message will be duplicated.
(Contributed by Noah Hertz Marks, age 7)

RULES

What Is Chametz?

What is *chametz* (**chah-MEYTS** or **CHUH-mets**)? It is the Hebrew word for any food that has leavened or risen, or to which yeast has been added, like everyday breads and cakes. Anything that contains or touches anything leavened is also called *chametz*.

All *chametz* must be removed from the house before Passover. In the homes of the most observant Jews, every corner is cleaned: all bedding, furniture, closets, drawers, rugs, floors . . . everything! The cooking utensils, pots and pans, dishware, glassware, and silverware are all changed, or else they must be completely *kashered* (cleaned and made kosher) especially for Passover. In Israel, special huge pots of water are set up in the streets to *kasher* the pots. Instead of doing all this work, many families keep separate sets of dishes, glasses, pots and pans, and utensils that they use only on Passover.

Why do we do all of this? In the Torah (in Exodus 12:15), we are

No chametz on Passover!
Leah Glass, age 12

Where is the chametz? Can you find the candle, the feather, and the dustpan?
Amsterdam Haggadah, Holland, 1723

told: "Even the first day you will put away the leaven out of your house." The Talmud (in *Pesahim*) tells us exactly how to do this. On the night before the seder, on the thirteenth of *Nisan*, all leaven in the house is gathered together. The father or head of the house conducts a search by the light of a wax candle, using a chicken feather to sweep the *chametz* into a bowl. This ceremony is called *"bedikat* (**be-dee-KAT**) *chametz,"* which is Hebrew for "searching for *chametz."* The family says this prayer:

בָּרוּךְ אַתָּה יְיָ, אֱלֹהֵינוּ מֶלֶךְ
הָעוֹלָם, אֲשֶׁר קִדְּשָׁנוּ בְּמִצְוֹתָיו
וְצִוָּנוּ עַל בִּעוּר חָמֵץ.

Baruch ata Adonai, Eloheinu melech ha-olam, asher kid'shanu b'mitsvotav v'tsivanu al bi-ur chameits.

Blessed are You, oh God, Ruler of the Universe, who makes us holy with Your *mitzvot* and calls us to remove leavened bread from our homes.

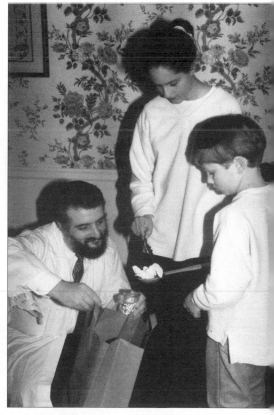

Using a feather, Megan pushes the chametz from the spoon into a paper bag.

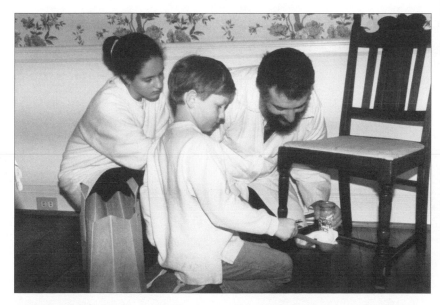

Father holds the candle as Sam scoops the chametz into the wooden spoon.

The following morning the last of the *chametz* is burned, given away, or "sold" to non-Jews with the help of a rabbi (since Jews are not permitted to own or possess *chametz* during the holiday) and then bought back after Passover.

So, if you want to get ready for your seder, start cleaning! And make sure to find all the *chametz!*

CUSTOMS

Searching for Chametz

You can make the search for *chametz* a fun game for your entire family. First, choose who gets to hide the *chametz*. The person who hides it has to make a list of where the pieces are hidden (to make sure they are all found!). Then take off on the great hunt! Sing a Passover song while you search, or make up an easy tune to hum while people are looking through the house so you'll know where everyone is!

An Afikoman Dustpan (from France)

Barbara's friend, Simone Lipman, was born in Alsace, a part of France. She remembers this custom from her family:

"Every year we hid a large piece of the *afikoman* in a drawer to bring us good luck throughout the year. But, by the next Passover, that *afikoman* piece became *chametz*. So, on the night before Passover when we searched for *chametz*, Father took a goose feather and swept the *chametz* in the house onto the *afikoman* piece. Then, they burned all the pieces together."

PROJECT

Spring Cleaning Tzedakah

Use "spring cleaning" time to sort through old clothes, toys, and garage items. You can donate them to people in need. And, you can give your *chametz* (leavened foods) to a food bank, a homeless shelter, or a soup kitchen. In that way, your food will help many other people!

SEDER TALK

Getting Rid of the "Chametz" in Our Lives

It feels so good to clean our homes before Passover. We get rid of the foods that have *chametz* (the things we are not supposed to eat during the holiday). Some rabbis suggest we use this time to think about the things in our lives that may not be good for us. What kinds of things can we get rid of in time for Passover?

Let's see . . . how about an old habit, like chewing fingernails or tapping on tables? How about an old attitude, like always saying "no" to a new idea before thinking about it?

The more "*chametz*" we can get rid of, the more room there can be for good new things and times!

FUN

A Special Chametz Riddle

Question: How many times of the year can we eat *challah* on Shabbat?

Answer: 51! No matter what days of the week *Pesach* falls on, it will always fall on only one Shabbat, and on that Shabbat we cannot eat *challah* because it is made with leavened bread.

Michael is looking for the chametz. Can you help him find it?

Cheryl Rush, age 7

INTRODUCTION

For thousands of years, Jews have read the story of Passover from the Haggadah *at their Passover seders. All other prayer books are considered sacred and are treated with special care, but the* Haggadah, *while sacred in its own way, is meant to be used and loved by everyone at the seder table.* Matzah *crumbs, wine stains, and turned-down pages tell the story of the people who have used it year after year. What are some stories of your* Haggadot?

"My own Haggadah cover."
Credit: Leah Glass, age 12

STORY

Some family *Haggadot* are precious treasures passed down from generation to generation. Here is a true story of what happened to a *Haggadah* long ago. It was told by Fred Hertz, who was a teenager in the city of Coesfeld, Germany, when the Nazis came to power.

The Haggadah That Traveled (from Germany)
by Fred Hertz

On the night of November 9 and the day of November 10, 1938, the Nazis tried to destroy everything Jewish in Germany. Many, many Jewish homes, synagogues, and businesses were looted. So much glass was shattered, that this terrible night was called the "Night of Broken Glass" or *Kristallnacht* in German.

At that time I was studying in a high school across the border in Holland. My parents were visiting another city. When we returned, we found the inside of our house destroyed. Even the sinks had been torn from the walls; water covered everything. The Nazis had taken what they could, and, with axes and hammers, they had destroyed the rest. My own treasures were either smashed or gone: my violin, my stamp collection, my camera, all the gifts that I had been given for my Bar Mitzvah.

From amidst this destruction, we began to put our house together, to seek out the treasures we could still

find. Thrown out with the debris was a small metal vase, about ten inches high, which was completely broken, like the pieces of a jigsaw puzzle. But the vase had been a gift from my father to my mother, and I could not bear to part with it. So I took the vase from the pile of garbage, brought it back to school in Holland, and kept it safe from further harm.

Among the rescued papers was a packet of love letters my great-grandparents had written to each other in Judeo-German, a special German-Jewish language using Hebrew letters to write German words. The letters had been written about one hundred years before and hidden inside a wall of the house for many, many years. And, among the other family treasures we found the Passover *Haggadot,* in Hebrew and in German, which had been in our family since they were printed, most of them more than one hundred years ago. My grandfather had used them every year at our family's seder. Everyone had a *Haggadah* to read from. After my grandfather died, my father used the same *Haggadot* every year. After the *Kristallnacht,* I took these *Haggadot* to Holland, across the border, to keep them safe for Passover seders in the future.

My parents had never thought of leaving Germany. After all, my family had been in Germany since 1492, when they were forced to leave their homes in Spain. But in 1939, when so many Jewish homes had been destroyed, they knew it was time to leave. But to where? Which countries would accept Jews? My parents received special permission to go to Palestine. Luckily, they left Germany just before World War II started in September 1939. They were not allowed to take any money. The things they decided to send by boat were later stolen by the Germans.

Since I was a good student, I was allowed to go to Palestine to study in the technical college there. So, when I graduated from my high school in Holland, I sent a box, with my favorite things, to Palestine. That

The Hertz family Haggadah.

Alison's Haggadah was created by her family (Cherie's family).

Benna reads the Haggadah that her mom got as a present when she was a child in Canada.

is how my great-grandparents' letters and the vase remained safe. Sometime later, after arriving in Israel, I put the vase together, piece by piece. And that is how the *Haggadot* remained safe, too. I kept them for the eighteen years that I lived in Israel. And I have them all until this very day and use them for our family's seders in Durham, North Carolina.

SEDER TALK

Where Does the Word Haggadah Come From?

The Hebrew word *Haggadah* comes from the word meaning "to tell." You might know other Hebrew words that sound nearly the same and which are related, like *aggadah* (a story from the Talmud), *l'hagid* (to tell), and *maggid* (one who teaches through stories).

Who Reads the Haggadah?

In ancient times, there were very few books, so the *seder* leader quite often read the *Haggadah* aloud. At most modern *seders*, everyone has a

Zöe and Anna practice reading the Haggadah.

Haggadah to read. At some seders, like the seders of the Jews from Yemen, everybody reads the *Haggadah* together in one loud voice. In other places, everyone takes turns reading. What's your favorite part of the *Haggadah* to read?

The Oldest Haggadah

The oldest *Haggadah* is more than one thousand years old!

The *Haggadah* has been written in dozens of languages and read all over the world. Even though all *Haggadot* tell the same basic story, the contents of the *Haggadah* have changed greatly throughout Jewish history. For instance, hundreds of years ago the *Haggadah* told the *entire* story of the life of Moses. It also included all the Passover prayers recited in synagogues, as well as information about ways to celebrate *Shavuot,* the next major Jewish holiday in the Jewish calendar. In modern times, *Haggadot* contain the Exodus story, songs, prayers, poetry, and even quotes from famous rabbis and other writers.

This 19th-century Sephardic Haggadah was used in Corfu, Greece!
Verona Haggadah, Italy, 1828

Many years ago, *Haggadot* were very much the same. But today there are thousands of versions of the *Haggadah.* Each one is a little different from the others.

A Haggadah for the Blind

Did you ever wonder how blind children read the *Haggadah?* They use a special *Haggadah,* printed in Braille, a system of raised dots for each Hebrew letter.

And where do they get these Braille *Haggadot?* From the Jewish Braille Institute of America, in New York, which has sent hundreds of *Haggadot* each *Pesach* to blind children and grown-ups all over the world for more than sixty years.

The Four Questions in Hebrew Braille.

SONG

History

Words & Music: Fran Avni

Soft Rock

His-to-ry___ is our sto-ry too___

It's no mys-te-ry that an-cient his-to-ry

ev-'ry-thing that's gone be-fore and used to be is all a-bout me and

you yes ev-'ry-thing that's gone be-fore and used to be is

all a-bout me and you cause ev-'ry year we sing the songs re-

tell the same old sto-ries___ of things that hap-pened

long a-go of her-oes and their glo-ries cause

Coda · D.C. 3x to ⊕ poi Coda

all a-bout you and all a-bout me and all a-bout me and you

We are all part of everything
That's gone before us
Yesterdays become tomorrows
Todays become tomorrows
Refrain

Coda
Everything that's gone before and used to be
Is all about me and you—'cause
Everything that's gone before and used to be
Is all about me and
All about you and
All about me and you.

The Hebrew letter "Vav" from the word U'rechatz—the washing of the hands.
Eisenstein Haggadah, U.S., 1928

The Hebrew letter "Koof" from the word kiddush—the blessing of the wine.
Eisenstein Haggadah, U.S., 1928

CRAFT

Illuminated Page of a Haggadah

The *Haggadah* is one of the few Jewish religious books that may be illustrated because it is not a sacred book like the Torah. Every artist has a different idea about how to picture the Exodus story. Many *Haggadot* show women playing an important role in the seder. One very old *Haggadah* shows all the people with the heads of birds, and others are illustrated with plants and animals instead of people. This is because the second commandment tells us not to make images of people.

A few hundred years ago in Europe, people made special illustrations for *Haggadot* by creating very fancy first letters for words in the *Haggadah*. They were large, had beautiful colored designs around them, and were painted with gold, which shone brightly. And so they were called "illuminated manuscripts." Create a page of illuminated manuscript of your favorite part of the seder, and keep it as a treasured part of your seders for years to come.

WHAT YOU NEED:

a large piece of heavy paper (light colored) or a piece of poster board, 8 1/2" x 11"
a piece of lined or unlined paper to practice on
ruler
pencil
thin marking pens or colored pencils
gold pen or gold paint and thin brush

WHAT YOU DO:

1. Choose a favorite part of the *Haggadah* to illustrate. Some good ideas are *"Dayenu," "Chad Gadya,"* the Ten Plagues, or the parting of the Reed Sea.

2. Decide which words to use (in Hebrew, English, or both) and write them out on a separate sheet of paper to practice writing them.

3. With the pencil, make a one-to-two-inch margin around the whole piece of heavy paper.

4. Draw the first letter of the first word on the heavy paper. Make a beautiful design around the letter in gold and other colors. Then write the rest of the words in beautiful script. Do this for the first letter in each paragraph or for the most important words.

5. When you have finished with the writing, make beautiful designs in the margin to frame the words. Use the colored pens or pencils to make pictures or designs of important things in the writing. The illumination brings the writing to life!

6. Hang your illuminated manuscript in the place where you are having your seder, or read from your page when you reach that part of your seder. Save your page, and add a new page for next year's seder.

MORE SEDER TALK

Where is Moses mentioned in the Haggadah?

(Here's a hint: Look in the part about the plagues!)

In a *Haggadah* used by many, many Jews in the United States, Moses is mentioned only once, in a verse taken from Exodus 14:31: "Israel saw the great hand of the Lord which He had laid upon Egypt; the people feared the Lord and they believed in the Lord and in His servant Moses."

An illuminated letter "Pey." Can you find the waves, eye, bricks, pyramids, sand, and palm trees?
Lisa Rauchwerger, Cutting Edge Creations

INTRODUCTION

The seder (the Hebrew word for "order") is the ceremony and meal that Jews conduct on the eve of Passover. Family and friends, who gather together to celebrate the holiday, follow a specific order of blessings and rituals that Jews have developed over thousands of years.

The seder plate, which sits on the table, holds the various symbols—karpas (greens), charoset (mortar for bricks), betzah (egg), zeroa (shank bone), and maror (bitter herbs)—that we talk about or over which we recite a blessing. The plate is usually made of china, glass, or pottery. It is divided into five or six sections, either by words or pictures for each item, or by individual small dishes that rest on the plate. Many seder plates are works of art, hand-painted, or professionally crafted, and they are often handed down in each family from generation to generation.

In this chapter you'll find out about different kinds of seders and the special symbols that are placed on the seder plate (the k'arah) and on the seder table to help Jews re-enact the drama of the Exodus story.

Barbara's seder plate from London shows the order of the seder.

STORY

What would you do if you were hundreds of miles away from your home on the night of Passover? How would you find a seder to attend? Long ago and far away, Yacov ben Yosef (**yah-KOVE ben yo-SEF**), the man in this story, had the very same problem. Do you think you could solve it in as clever a way?

Radishes for the Seder

A Sephardic historical tale by Barbara Rush

The year was 1489. In a small city in northern Spain on the day before *Pesach*, Yacov ben Yosef walked the streets of the town, not noticing the warm sunshine or the beautiful flowers. Yacov's mind was on his own troubles.

FIND A MAP OF WESTERN EUROPE. CAN YOU LOCATE THE DIFFERENT COUNTRIES THAT YACOV WENT TO?

Who was Yacov ben Yosef, and why was he so miserable? You see, Yacov ben Yosef was a trader who lived in Germany, far to the north. More than one month before, he had taken dyes and spices that he had brought from countries in the east, loaded them on his horse-drawn wagon, and traveled to the city of Amsterdam in Holland. There, he boarded a ship that would take him and his precious cargo to Lisbon in Portugal, where he had always sold his merchandise for a good price. Yes, his spices were dearly loved in Lisbon. Perhaps this time they would even reach the kitchens of the royal palace!

The journey should have taken four weeks, which was a long time for a young man like Yacov ben Yosef to be away from his family and to be sailing on the open sea. But such was the life of Yacov ben Yosef and many other Jewish men who made their living by selling dyes and spices in the countries of western Europe. Because he would be away from home during Passover, Yacov had made arrangements to spend the holiday with Jewish friends in Lisbon.

So what was Yacov doing in Spain? The boat, you see, was driven forward only by the force of the wind in its sails, and for the last week the wind had been weak and quiet. The boat could not go forward. So the captain had decided to head for shore in the north of Spain, and to wait there until the winds were stronger.

And, why was Yacov so unhappy? True, he could not get to Lisbon in time for the seder. But couldn't he celebrate *Pesach* in Spain? Couldn't he go to a synagogue, where certainly a Jewish family would invite him to their seder? The answer is no! For the Christian king and queen of Spain had decided that all Jews had to become Christians too—or they would be killed. Many Jews did, indeed, convert. These New Christians, as they were called, prayed in the church, bought pork

Rosie Jablonsky, age 11

in the market, and acted in every way like other Christians around them. But many did not forget that they were Jews. They thought of themselves as "secret Jews"—Christians in public and Jews in secret. And so they built secret rooms in their houses where they could pray together, sing on the Sabbath, and have a seder for *Pesach*.

Of course, they had to be very careful that no one saw or heard them. The king and queen sent spies to watch these New Christians. If the spies noticed them cleaning their houses on Friday afternoon, or did not see them buying pork in the market nor see smoke coming through their chimneys on Saturday, they might be found out. And their punishment would be death!

So now you can understand why no one invited Yacov to a seder. In this strange land there was no synagogue, no way to find a fellow Jew. Yacov knew how dangerous it was for a Jew to be caught.

"Well," he said to himself, "if I can't find a seder on *Pesach,* I'll make one myself. I'll go to the market and buy greens for *karpas,* and an egg, and a radish for *maror,* and, perhaps, even a bone." He did not dare think of how to get *matzot.*

At the market Yacov saw luscious vegetables, meat of all kinds hung on hooks, and platters of sweet fruits dried in the sun. First, he bought some oranges—Yacov was very hungry—and then he began to purchase, one by one, the things he needed for his seder. The greens were no problem, nor was the egg. But when he approached the radish seller, Yacov noticed that many other people had come to buy radishes too. So Yacov stood there waiting his turn. As he did so, Yacov closed his eyes and pictured the seder at home, where, following the order of the *Haggadah,* each person must eat a slice of the crisp bitter radish and a spoonful of sweet *charoset,* sandwiched between two small pieces of *matzot.* Oh, how Yacov wished he

Rosie Jablonsky, age 11

were back home with his family! Opening his eyes, Yacov saw that now there were even more people crowded around the radish seller. "Why do so many people want radishes?" he thought to himself. "You would think they're all having a seder!"

And then, in a flash, he had an idea: "That's it! The people are buying radishes for their seder! I'll follow someone home to see what happens." After Yacov paid for his radishes, he followed a woman, with her bunches of radishes, down many narrow streets and

Sally Jablonsky, age 10

through a maze of alleys. Was she weaving through the streets to confuse someone who might be following her? Or was this just Yacov's imagination? At last she disappeared through a door in a courtyard.

Yacov did not dare appear in daylight for the spies of the king and queen might be watching, so he waited till dark. Then he crossed the courtyard and knocked at the door. His heart pounded. Was this a Jewish home? Did he dare say he was a Jew? Would they let him enter? Yacov had to put his faith in heaven. He had to take a chance.

The door opened. There stood the woman Yacov had seen at the market. She glanced at Yacov, then disappeared, only to return a moment later with her husband. For a moment the couple stood in silence.

Yacov could not think of the right words to say. What words would make the couple know that he was a Jew? And what words would prove to him that they were Jewish? Then, suddenly, Yacov spoke—in the best Spanish he knew: "All the people are responsible for each other." These words were almost like the words of the Talmud he had studied at home: "All Israel are responsible for one another." If this husband and wife were Jewish, they would understand that he was a fellow Jew.

As Yacov spoke, he held out the items he had bought at the market: the egg, cradled warmly in his pocket, the greens, and, last of all, the radishes. Without a word, the husband smiled a quick smile and

Polishing the silver candlesticks.

motioned for Yacov to follow. Then the man touched a spring behind a tapestry on the wall. A panel slid open. The three hurried through. Quickly they climbed down a secret staircase. At the bottom was a hall that led to a secret room underneath the main floor of the house. That door too slid open, and there, inside the room, were a dozen people—men, women, and children—seated around a table. On the table were an egg, a bone, greens, *charoset,* and a bunch of radishes.

That year Yacov ben Yosef did not have to celebrate *Pesach* by himself. Far from home he had found his fellow Jews—and a Passover seder.

BLESSINGS

There are so many things that we have to be thankful for at Passover: freedom, spring, renewal, the Exodus. And there are so many things to bless at the seder! In fact, there are over four times four (sixteen!) blessings at the first seder—for everything from candle-lighting to *karpas!* Actually, the blessings start the night before the seder with the prayer for searching for the *chametz.*

Blessings traditionally begin with the words:

ברוך אתה יי אלהינו מלך העולם
Baruch atah Adonai, Elohenu melech Ha'olam . . .
Blessed are you, God, ruler of the universe . . .

On Passover, we recite some of the same blessings that we recite on Shabbat and other holidays, as well as several special blessings. We begin the seder by lighting the festival candles and reciting the *Shehekhiyanu,* a blessing giving thanks that we have arrived at this moment, this day, and this season. The special blessings take different forms and are said at different times during the seder.

- Blessing the children: After the *Shehekhiyanu* is recited, some people bless their children with the words from the priestly blessing: "May God bless you and keep you. May God's face shine upon you. May God be gracious to you and grant you peace."
- Blessing over the wine: We say this blessing four times in the seder, one for each of the four cups of wine.
- Blessing over the *karpas,* the green vegetable.

LVS, age 15

- *Rachtzah,* the blessing recited over the washing of one's hands.
- *Motzi,* the blessing recited over *matzah,* as bread.
- Blessing over the *matzah,* as Passover unleavened bread.
- Blessing over the *maror,* the bitter herb.
- Four blessings of the *birkat hamazon,* the grace after meals.

Indeed, we are thankful for many, many things.

SEDER TALK

Other Hebrew Words that Sound Like "Seder"

The word seder is the Hebrew word for "order." It comes from the Hebrew verb *"l'sa-der,"* which means "to straighten out" or "put in order," like when you straighten your room if it's messy.

Here are four other words that sound like the word "seder:"

- *siddur:* the Hebrew word for the prayer book. The prayers follow a certain order.
- *sidrah:* the Hebrew word for the Torah portion that is read each week in the synagogue. The Torah portions are read in the order they appear in the Torah.
- *sadar:* the Hebrew word for a man who is a typesetter. He puts the letters of the alphabet in the proper order in each printed word.
- *b'seder:* the Hebrew word that means "it's okay" or "everything's in order."

Do you know any other Hebrew words that sound like "seder"?

THE ORDER OF THE SEDER

The traditional order of the seder is:

KADESH: the reciting of the *kiddush,* the blessing of the wine

U'RECHATZ: the washing of the hands

KARPAS: the blessing over the green vegetable

YACHATZ: the breaking of the middle *matzah*

MAGGID: the telling of the Exodus story

RACHTZAH: the washing of the hands before the meal

MOTZI MATZAH: the blessing over the *matzah* and the prayer before eating

MAROR: the blessing over the bitter herbs

KORECH: the Hillel sandwich of *matzah, maror,* and *charoset*

SHULHAN ORECH: the festive meal

TZAFUN: the *afikoman*

BARECH: the saying of grace

HALLEL: the psalms of praise

NIRTZAH: the conclusion of the seder

"Let's have a practice seder."

CUSTOM
How Many Seders Are There?

In Israel the seder is celebrated on only one night. In other parts of the world some Jews have one seder, many other Jews have two seders (on the first two nights of Passover), and some even have three.

What is the third seder for? The first seder and, for many people, the second seder also, is for family and friends. Sometimes, a group that has a common interest might gather for another seder during the "in between days," the *chol ha'moed* (**choll-hah-MO-ed**). This may be a group in your synagogue, club, or organization. You can never have too many seders!

THE SYMBOLS OF THE SEDER PLATE
KARPAS, THE GREEN VEGETABLE

LVS, age 15

The very first food eaten at the seder is the *karpas* (**CAR-pahs**), the green vegetable. It is meant to remind us of long ago, when the Jews were slaves in Egypt. God sent the tenth plague—the killing of the first-born—and the Children of Israel were saved because they marked the doorposts of their houses with the blood of a sacrificed lamb.

What does that have to do with the *karpas* on the seder plate? You see, the Children of Israel placed the blood from the lamb on their doorposts with a tall, green plant called hyssop (**HISS-op**). The *karpas* reminds us of this plant.

KARPAS CUSTOMS
KARPAS AROUND THE WORLD

Some Jews use lettuce . . . or parsley . . . or celery. Why?

In Israel, celery is often used because one of the Hebrew words for celery is *karpas!* Any kind of "bunched" or leafy plant may be used as long as it is green. In some homes Jews (especially those of Sephardic background) use scallions, which are green onions, because green is the color of growing grass, of nature's rebirth, of new life in the spring!

We dip the *karpas* into water that has salt, vinegar, or lemon juice in it. Then we recite a blessing before eating the food, just as we do for all the food and drink that we consume at the seder. Some say the water is bitter, just as the lives of our ancestors were bitter as slaves. Others say the salt water reminds us of the tears our ancestors shed over their harsh lives.

Watch out, though, if you use vinegar! It can make your tongue burn. But that's the idea! The *karpas* is supposed to "bite" your tongue to keep you awake and curious about what will happen next in the seder!

KARPAS SNACKS

This is a good time to pass around a pretty tray of bite-sized pieces of celery, lettuce, and other green "veggies." These snacks will satisfy your hunger until more food is served later in the seder.

MAROR, THE BITTER HERB

Maror (**mah-ROAR**) is the bitter herb. In Yiddish it is called *chrain* (**chrane**). Many Ashkenazic Jews use horseradish for *maror*, either whole, sliced, or ground up into a dip. But not everybody uses horseradish. There are lots of possibilities!

Hyssop

MAROR CUSTOMS

FOUR SPECIAL MAROR TRADITIONS

1. Yemenite Jews use romaine lettuce as their bitter herb. They scatter the lettuce leaves all over the seder table as a reminder that our lives as slaves were filled with much bitterness.

LVS, age 15

2. Jews in Gibraltar use their own special food for *maror*: artichokes!
3. In some parts of the Balkans, the seder guests throw pieces of *maror* on the floor to show that we should throw away the bitterness of slavery!
4. During the Holocaust Jewish prisoners in concentration camps used pieces of potatoes as their bitter herb since potatoes were one of the few foods they had to eat. Today some Jews use a potato for *maror* to remember the Jews who lived during the Holocaust.

STILL MORE MAROR CUSTOMS

Some seder plates have two places for horseradish. Why?

Some people display the *maror*—the ground horseradish or the green top from horseradish—in one place, but use *maror* from the second place as the bitter herb in the *matzah* sandwich, called the Hillel Sandwich (named for the famous first-century Rabbi). It is made with the bitter herbs and *charoset* placed between two small pieces of *matzah*.

Try to find the strongest horseradish root for your seder. It will really clear out your nose!!

Judy Lande Haran

CHAROSES OR CHAROSET, THE SWEET MORTAR

It doesn't matter if you're an Ashkenazic Jew who calls it *charoses* or a Sephardic Jew who calls it *charoset*. The mixture of nuts and fruits reminds all Jews of the mortar that the Israelites used to make the bricks for Pharaoh's buildings. Usually, *charoset* is made with fruits and nuts from Israel, mixed with cinnamon. Each Jewish community makes its own special kind of *charoset*.

- Jews from Iraq use date syrup and almonds to make their *charoset*.
- Guess what Jews from Yemen use? Hot chili pepper!
- Jews from Eastern Europe usually chop apples and nuts into a chunky mixture.
- Sephardic and Oriental Jews use spices and dates and other fruits to make a sticky, sweeter mixture. Sometimes they use fruit saved from the last holiday of *Sukkot*. And sometimes they roll the sticky *charoset* into little balls, and serve two or three balls to each guest.

CHAROSET SEDER TALK

Question: Why is there no blessing for the *charoset*?

Answer: *Charoset* was not used in the ancient seders. Then, in later times, the Rabbis added it to the celebration as a part of the eating of *matzah* and *maror*. So it does not have a separate blessing.

Question: Why is *charoset* sweet?

Answer: The *charoset* is a reminder of the bitterness of slavery. But, the taste is sweet! Why? Maybe it is to suggest that even in the bitterest times we can still hope for a sweet future.

DURING WORLD WAR II, WHEN SOLDIERS COULD NOT MAKE CHAROSET, THEY PUT A WHOLE BRICK ON THE SEDER TABLE AS A REMINDER OF THE BRICKS THE JEWS MADE IN EGYPT!

FIVE FAVORITE CHAROSET RECIPES

There is no one recipe for *charoset*. Search any Jewish cookbook, or ask any Jewish cook, and you'll find many different recipes from different parts of the world. Here are some of our favorites.

Barbara's Charoses: A Recipe from Eastern Europe

Barbara's mother taught her to make *charoses* when she was a little girl. This is the way Barbara taught her children, Avi and David, to make *charoses*. Now their children—Barbara's grandchildren—make it the same way. This recipe makes 10–12 servings.

YOU WILL NEED:

2 red apples
about 1 cup sweet red wine or grape juice
1 cup chopped walnuts (buy the walnuts already
    shelled and chopped into pieces)
paring knife for peeling apples
wooden bowl
metal chopping blade
measuring cup
large spoon for stirring

*"Happy chopping and happy tasting!"
from Seth and Cheryl.*

WHAT YOU DO:

1. Carefully peel the apples and cut them length-wise in half and then in half again. Carefully cut away the core from each slice. Discard the peels and cores.
2. Put the peeled and cored apples into a wooden bowl. Ask an adult to show you how to use the chopping blade to chop the apples into pieces the size of your thumbnail.
3. Add the chopped nuts to the bowl with the chopped apples.
4. Measure 1 cup of red wine or grape juice and pour it into the apple and nut mixture.
5. Stir the mixture until it becomes the color of the wine or juice. Now the charoses is ready to eat—or you can sprinkle it with cinnamon.

Cherie's Charoses:
A Recipe from England

Cherie's grandmother, Rae Olesh, who came to America from England, made the same basic recipe as Barbara's, but used hazelnuts (filberts) instead of walnuts. And, instead of sprinkling just cinnamon into the mix, she liked to mix 1 teaspooon of cinnamon *and* 1 tablespoon of sugar together and mix well. This recipe makes 10–12 servings.

Danielle's Charoset:
A Recipe from Singapore

Three-year-old Danielle Cohen, who lives in North Carolina, loves this recipe because it's so sweet. Her grandparents first tasted the *charoset* made from this recipe at the seder of a Jewish Iranian family in Singapore. This recipe makes 12–15 servings.

WHAT YOU NEED:

Note: You may find some of these ingredients (like dates, walnuts, and almonds) already chopped. If not, chop them into small, bite-size pieces.

1 cup dried figs
1 cup dried apricots
1 cup pitted dates, chopped
1/2 cup walnuts, chopped
1/2 cup almonds, chopped or slivered
1/2 cup golden raisins
1/2 teaspoon grated orange peel (you can buy
    this in a bottle)
2 tablespoons honey
1 cup orange juice (as needed)
large wooden chopping board
large mixing bowl
grater
large spoon for stirring
metal chopping blade
measuring spoons
measuring cup

WHAT YOU DO:

1. Ask an adult to show you how to chop up the figs and apricots on the wooden chopping board. Then put the figs, apricots, and dates in the mixing bowl.
2. Add the walnuts and almonds to the mixing bowl with the dates, figs, and apricots.
3. Add the golden raisins, the grated orange peel, and the honey to the mixture.
4. Stir the mixture until the ingredients are evenly spread around. Leave the mixture overnight in the refrigerator so the flavors have time to blend together.
5. The next day test the mixture. If it tastes too dry, gradually add some or all of the orange juice.

Seemah Mares's Charoset (from Rangoon)

Seemah Mares comes from Rangoon, Burma, in Southeast Asia, where *charoset* is made from date syrup and walnuts. It can take hours to make! This is an easy-to-make version of her Rangoon *charoset*. Although this recipe is simple, it does require boiling water, so please ask an adult to help you! This recipe makes 15 servings.

WHAT YOU NEED:

1/2 pound pitted dates
2 quarts water
5 ounces chopped walnuts (buy
    the walnuts already shelled
    and chopped)
large pot
colander
blender

Judy Lande Haran

WHAT YOU DO:

1. Pour water into a pot, cover the pot, and put it on the stove to boil.
2. When the water is boiling, add the dates and simmer them, with the lid partially covering the pot, until they are very tender. It will take about an hour.

3. When the dates can be mashed easily with a fork, they are tender. Ask an adult to help you pour the water and dates through the colander. Don't forget to turn off the burner!

4. Blenders can be dangerous, so pour the drained dates into the blender *before you plug it in.* Remember to put the lid on the blender, then plug it in and set it on "puree." You'll know you're done blending when the dates have turned to syrup.

5. Unplug the blender and pour the syrup back into the pot.

6. Pour the chopped nuts into the pot with the date syrup.

7. Stir well and serve at room temperature.

A Charoset Pyramid: A Recipe from North Carolina

Barbara's friend, Vicky Hertz, who lives in Durham, N.C., says: "Since the *charoset* symbolizes the mortar that the Israelites used to build the pyramids, it seemed only logical to make it look like a pyramid. I created this *charoset* pyramid about ten or twelve years ago when my twin boys were very little. Now they help me make it every Passover." Because this recipe requires the use of a blender or food processor, be sure to have an adult help you.

A charoset pyramid

WHAT YOU NEED:

2 small apples
1 orange
8 oz. pitted dates
3 oz. dried apricots or raisins
1 cup walnut or almond pieces (buy the nuts already shelled and
    chopped)
 2 teaspoons cinnamon
1$\frac{1}{2}$ cups whole almonds for the outside
honey (optional)
wooden bowl
metal chopper
food processor or blender
knife
spatula
shallow baking pan

WHAT YOU DO:

1. Peel the apples and cut them in half along the core. Cut them in half again and cut out the core from each apple slice. Put the quartered apples in a wooden bowl.
2. Peel the orange, break it into sections, and add it to the bowl.
3. Add the pitted dates, dried apricots or raisins, and chopped walnuts or almonds to the wooden bowl.
4. Use a metal chopper to chop the fruit and nuts.
5. Scrape the chopped mixture into a food processor or blender. Remember not to plug it in until *after* you have scraped in the mixture. Add the cinnamon and grind the fruit and nuts until you have a fine, sticky mixture.
6. Mound the mixture on a plate. If it doesn't stick together, add a tiny bit of honey. Use a wide spatula to form the mixture into the shape of a pyramid.
7. Roast the whole almonds: Spread the almonds in a shallow pan and put it in a pre-heated oven or toaster oven for five minutes at 350 degrees. Wait until the almonds cool before doing the next step.
8. Starting at the bottom of the pyramid, gently press rows of roasted almonds into the *charoset,* as shown in the illustration.

Vicky adds, "The only problem you may have with this pyramid is getting people to 'ruin' the pyramid in order to eat it." She also says, "Now that I've been making this *charoset* in the shape of a pyramid, *charoset* in a bowl looks boring."

FUN

A Nut Game

Nuts aren't just for *charoset.* On Passover, many games are played with nuts, too. Cherie remembers playing "marbles" with hazelnuts. She placed a walnut as a target at one end of a hallway, and rolled the hazelnuts one at a time, taking turns with the other players, to try and hit the walnut. Whoever hit the walnut got all of the nuts!

Who will win the hazelnut game?

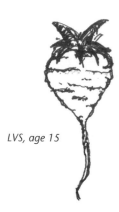

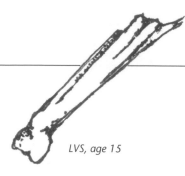

LVS, age 15

LVS, age 15

ZEROA, THE SHANKBONE AS A REMINDER OF SACRIFICE

The *zeroa* (**zeh-ROH-ah**), shankbone, part of the lower leg of a lamb, is a symbol of the animal sacrifices that were made in ancient times. Sometimes it's hard to find a lamb shankbone, especially since many Jews do not eat lamb on Passover. So, another kind of bone can be used, such as the leg bone of a chicken.

If you or your family are vegetarians, you don't need to worry. You can use a beet on the seder plate because it's red and it "bleeds" like the blood of an animal.

ZEROA SEDER TALK

Question: How is the shankbone different from all of the other symbols on the seder plate?

Answer: The shankbone is not held up, it is not blessed, and it is not eaten.

Question: So why do we have it on the seder plate at all?

Answer: The shankbone is a reminder of the sacrifice of the lamb, whose blood was used on the doorposts of Jewish homes to save the Jews from the tenth plague, the killing of the firstborn. It may also serve as a reminder of how God took us out of Egypt with a "strong hand and an outstretched arm."

Question: Why don't we bless, eat, or even point to the shankbone during the seder?

Answer: In ancient times, paschal lambs were offered as sacrifices in the Holy Temple. Since the destruction of the Temple in 70 C.E., there have been no more sacrifices. So we have the bone on the plate as a reminder of the sacrifice, but we do not give it special attention or eat it.

MORE ZEROA SEDER TALK

The shankbone is a reminder of the "outstretched arm" of God. Maybe it can also be a reminder of how we can reach out to each other: to comfort

ZEROA CUSTOM (FROM AFGHANISTAN)

Jews in Afghanistan used to keep the roasted shankbone from their seder plate in the dining room all year long for good luck!

one another, to help each other, to offer friendship and love, and to create peace.

BETZAH, THE EGG FOR NEW LIFE

The *betzah* (**beh-TSAH**), egg, on the seder plate symbolizes spring and new life. But it is burned, too, as a reminder of the difficult times of enslavement. It may also serve as a reminder of the Temple sacrifices. At many seders, each person dips a hard-boiled egg in a bowl of water mixed with salt, vinegar, or lemon juice.

BETZAH CUSTOMS

FOUR EGG TRADITIONS

- Jews from Libya place an egg on the seder plate for every child at the seder!
- Jews from Alsace-Lorraine in France still dye their eggs a warm shade of brown.
- In some families an egg is given to the child who asks the Four Questions.
- And, in Morocco, Jews cook the egg in hot water with onion skins so that the egg turns a deep reddish-brown, perhaps as a reminder of the Nile River turning red with blood.

LVS, age 15

BETZAH RECIPE

Red Eggs (from the Sephardic tradition)

Would you like to make red eggs for your seder, as do the Jews from Greece?

WHAT YOU NEED:

6 eggs
onion skins from 4 large red onions
2 tea bags of black tea
2-quart pot or deep pan
water
long-handled spoon or ladle
large bowl

WHAT YOU DO:

1. Place the raw eggs carefully into the pot.
2. Add enough water to cover the eggs.
3. Peel the onions and place the skins in the pot.
4. Add the tea bags to the pot.
5. Place the pot on the stove and heat the water until it boils. Here's a hint: putting the lid on the pot will make the water boil faster. But be sure to *remove* the lid once the water starts to boil!
6. Keep the pot boiling lightly for 20 minutes.
7. After 20 minutes are up, turn off the burner. Using the long-handled spoon or ladle, take out the eggs, place them in a large bowl, and rinse them in cool water.
8. Let the eggs cool before putting them in the refrigerator.

You can instead make just one egg for your seder plate. After boiling the egg, you can put it in the oven (along with other Passover foods that are baking). When the egg is brown, remove it from the oven and let it cool before placing it on your seder plate.

SEDER TALK

Seder Plate Symbols

There is no one correct way of placing the different symbols on the seder plate. Many seder plates have the names of each symbol written in Hebrew or English right on the plate to help you find the right place for each symbol, but many others do not. If your seder plate has no names written on it, don't worry. You may decide how to arrange your seder plate.

CUSTOM

No Seder Plate! (from Yemen and the Caucasus Mountains)

Guess what? In Yemenite tradition, there were no seder plates at all. In Yemen Jews put their Passover symbols right on the table! When it was time to raise the seder plate, everyone lifted the low table up in the air!

Cherie's seder plate from Turkey, with separate bowls.

In Israel today, most Yemenite families use a seder plate instead of the table.

In the Caucasus Mountains in Europe, the Jews lived far away from other people, and even from other Jews. It was very hard to get any fresh food for their seder plates. So they did the next best thing: they embroidered a seder plate with pictures of all of the seder items onto their tablecloths! That way, they could preserve the "seder plate" from year to year!

POEM

The Seder Plate Checklist

Hurry now, it's getting late.
Is everything on our seder plate?
Let's look and see:

Lettuce, celery, crispy, crunchy;
Cut some up for a *karpas* munchy!

Bitter herbs we call *maror*
Remind us that we're slaves no more.

Chopped *charoset*, oh so sweet
With nuts and apples, such a treat!

A bone to look at, not to eat
Or, instead, you may use a beet.

An egg for new life as spring nears
With salty water, reminds us of tears.

Karpas, maror, egg, bone, *charoset*—
So now our seder plate is all set!

Leah Glass, age 12

CRAFTS

A Stenciled Seder Plate Symbols Tablecloth

How beautiful the seder table looks with the seder plate, *matzot*, wine cups, and candles. You can help make it look even more beautiful by creating a special seder plate symbols tablecloth.

(continued on p. 87)

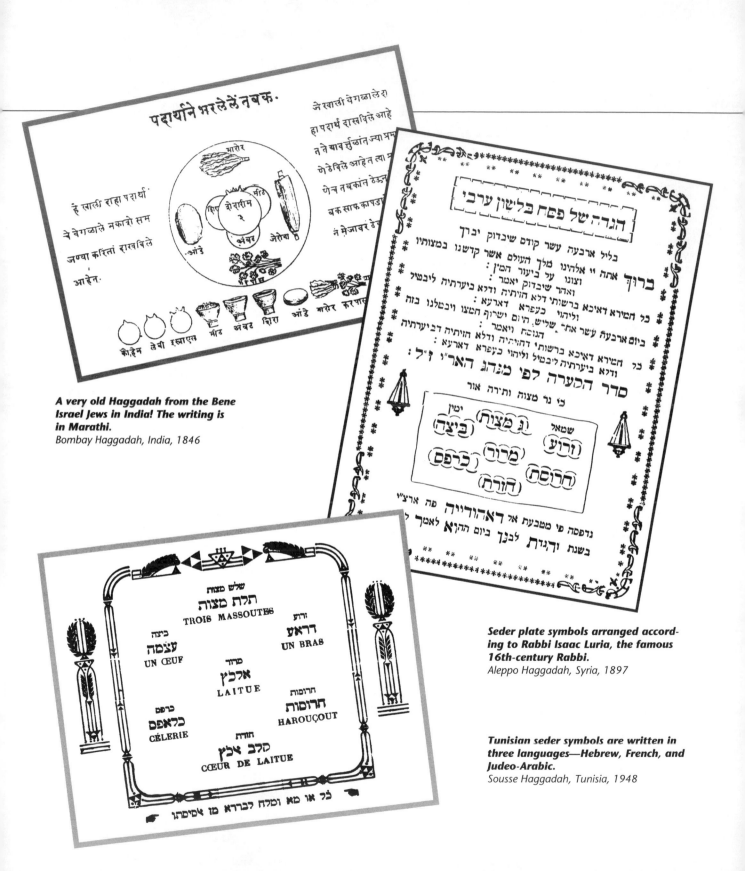

A very old Haggadah from the Bene Israel Jews in India! The writing is in Marathi.
Bombay Haggadah, India, 1846

Seder plate symbols arranged according to Rabbi Isaac Luria, the famous 16th-century Rabbi.
Aleppo Haggadah, Syria, 1897

Tunisian seder symbols are written in three languages—Hebrew, French, and Judeo-Arabic.
Sousse Haggadah, Tunisia, 1948

WHAT YOU NEED:

empty cereal box (or other thin cardboard)
carbon paper (to transfer the shapes onto the cardboard)
ball point pen
4 paper clips
small, pointed scissors
cookie sheet (make sure it's okay with your parents to use the
    cookie sheet because you are going to be covering it with paint)
stiff paint brush, 1 inch wide
acrylic textile paint (you can buy the paint at a craft store)
white sheet or tablecloth to fit your table
white piece of paper to practice on

WHAT YOU DO:

1. Photocopy page 88.
2. Place the carbon paper on the cardboard with the inked side down (away from you).
3. Put the photocopied stencil page on top of the carbon paper and secure the three sheets (cardboard, carbon paper, and photocopy) with a few paper clips.
4. Trace the outlines of the symbols, the broken lines separating the symbols, and the X marks at the center of the symbols. Press hard with the ball point pen so that the lines are completely transferred.
5. Using your scissors, cut the cardboard along the broken lines to separate the symbols. Then cut out the insides of the shapes. Push the scissors in at the X and cut from the inside out to the edges of each shape. The cardboard rectangles with the cut-out shapes are your stencils.
6. Put about 1/2 teaspoon of different colored textile paints on a cookie sheet—to make a palette. The paint will be thick.
7. Practice using the brush to dab the paint through the holes in the cardboard stencils onto the sheet of paper. Press the stencil against the paper with one hand while you make short, poking brush strokes with the other. Be sure to wash the brush between color changes.
8. When you have practiced enough, do the same thing onto the cloth. Spread the cloth on a large, flat surface such as a kitchen or

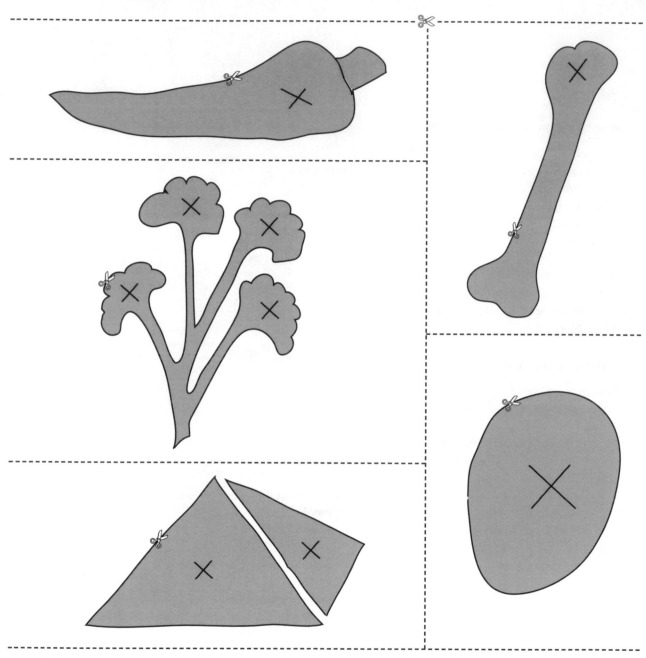

Joan Cohen

basement floor. (Do not do this project in a carpeted room.) Place the stencils near the edges of your cloth and dab on the paint. Repeat this step until you have a colorful, decorative border, but be careful not to smear your painted shapes as you work around the edge of the cloth. Alternate shapes and colors for variety.

A Hamsa (or Hand) Seder Plate

Some people in your community may not have enough money for their own seder plate. You can make a special seder plate and really "lend a hand!" (The hand, a symbol of protection and good luck for Jews and Arabs in the Middle East, is called a *hamsa,* the Arabic word for five.)

WHAT YOU NEED:

a light-colored plate (it can be paper, foam, or even ceramic)
non-toxic magic markers or paints and a paint brush

WHAT YOU DO:

1. Place the plate on a table.
2. Place your hand in the middle of the plate and trace with the marker or paint brush around the outline of your hand.
3. Draw a picture of one seder item for each finger of the hand (*charoset, maror, egg, shankbone, parsley*).
4. Write the word Passover in English and/or *Pesach* in Hebrew in the center of the hand.

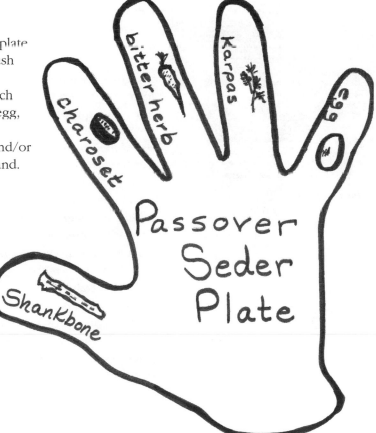

INTRODUCTION

Matzah, matzah, *and more* matzah! *Think of Passover, and you think of Jews eating* matzah—*tons of* matzah—*all over the world. That's a lot of* matzah! *(And more than one* matzah *is called* matzot.*)*

Matzah *is the flat, unleavened bread Jews eat on Passover. When our ancestors in Egypt were trying to escape in a hurry, they had no time to let the bread that they were baking rise. So, they ate flat, unleavened bread during their Exodus from* Mitzrayim. *As a reminder, we are commanded in the book of Exodus to eat* matzah *for seven days.*

In our time, most people buy their matzot *from the store, but some people still make them. Not too many years ago, everyone made his or her* matzot *for* Pesach.

For hundreds of years most matzot were round. In some countries, matzot were thick like pita, while in other places, they were thin and crisp. Usually, families baked their own, but people used community ovens, too, where everyone could bake together.

Matzah *must be mixed and baked within eighteen minutes because after eighteen minutes the water in the dough will cause the* matzah *to leaven or rise.*

There were many different ways of baking matzah:

Many Sephardic women baked matzah while singing songs and reciting poetry. This helped them work quickly. But in Libya, women were silent as they baked, and they wore a handkerchief over their mouths while preparing the matzot. They believed that by not talking to each other, they worked more quickly.

In some Sephardic communities men recited the Aleph Bet א, ב, ג, ד (aleph, bet, gimel, daled . . .) while making matzah. They believed that this added holiness to the matzot.

Until this day some Jews bake a kind of matzah called shmureh matzah. The name comes from the Hebrew word shomer, "guard." This

"I love matzah."

Can you tell what the hand is holding? A piece of matzah! This picture is used in many early Sephardic Haggadot.
Verona Haggadah, Italy, 1828, copied from the Venice Haggadah, 1609

Lots of Matzah **8**

Putting the shmureh matzah in an oven in Brooklyn, NY.

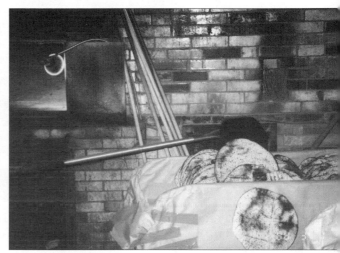

Shmureh matzah fresh out of the oven.

means that the wheat is specially guarded while it is growing. After the wheat is cut, no dampness or water may get into it. And the utensils used to make the matzah must be free from chametz.

Is there a matzah bakery in your city? Perhaps your religious school can arrange a trip there for you to see how matzot are made.

On the seder table, we place a plate with three matzot representing the Kohanim, the Levites, and the Israelites—the three branches of the Jewish people during the time of the Holy Temple. These matzot are covered with a napkin or a special matzah cover. Matzah covers come from many places and times throughout Jewish history. Some are plain, and some are very fancy.

At the early part of the seder, after the three matzot are shown, the seder leader breaks the middle of the three matzot. One half, called the afikoman, is placed in a cloth cover (like a napkin) or an envelope-like pocket, and is hidden.

The word afikoman may come from the Greek word for games, songs, and dances after a meal. Or, it might mean the dessert that is eaten after a feast. That is the meaning that Jews today give the afiko-

Barbara's matzah plate.

man *in our seders. Indeed, the* afikoman *is the last thing we eat at the seder*.

STORY

This is a story about a very special *matzah* cover.

The Matzah Cover That Saved a Life
A folktale from Syria, retold by Barbara Rush

Not long ago in Syria, in a small town near the country's capital of Damascus, a community of Jews tried to follow as best they could the *mitzvot* (**mihtz-VOTE** or **MITZ-vos**), the commandments of the Torah. The leader of the Jews was a rabbi, who had a beautiful, dark-eyed daughter. Her name was Sarah, and she was clever as well as beautiful.

Her favorite pastime was embroidering, a skill she learned from her mother and all her aunts. While the other girls spent time at games or childish play, Sarah sat with her needle and thread, creating embroideries that were rare in beauty. As the years passed, her sewing grew even more skillful, the embroideries more beautiful.

One day, shortly after the holiday of *Purim,* Sarah went into the woods and followed a trail into the meadow beyond to gather flowers to serve as a picture for her new embroidery. As she entered the meadow, she heard the rumble of horses' hooves. It was a band of thieves! They snatched her up, flowers and all, and took her to caves high in the mountains where they made their home.

There they told her that they would train her as a dancer and force her to dance for money in the streets of the neighboring towns. "Yes," they thought, "we can get good money for a dancing beauty such as this one." Sarah's heart fell. She wanted to cry. Instead, she swallowed the bread and drank from the cup her captors offered her, for she was hungry and thirsty after the long ride. Then she turned to the thieves and said, "Oh yes, I could learn to dance. But I know a skill that could earn ten times the money I would bring you as a dancer. You see, I know how to sew beautiful embroideries. They will bring high prices in the shops of the town."

"Can this really be true?" asked the thieves of each other. At last, they decided, "Why not give the girl a chance to prove her words?"

"Very well," they said to her, "we will bring you fine threads and fine cloth, and we will give you one week to sew your embroidery. If we are not satisfied, you will join the other girls as a dancer."

Then the thieves brought her fine white cloth, needles, and threads of silk and cotton in every color of the rainbow. For one week they left Sarah alone. She sewed from sunrise to sunset, day after day, stopping only to eat weak, watery soup and thin slices of bread, which the thieves left for her.

How magnificent her embroidery was! It contained patterns of flowers and green leaves, just like the flowers of the forest. It had strange designs, both curved and straight, set between the flowers all around the cloth. Sarah, you see, had made a cover for the *matzah,* the special flat bread her family ate on *Pesach.* In the middle of the lovely flowers and leaves, she had embroidered the word *matzah.*

When the week was up, the kidnappers came to see her work. They blinked in amazement. How magnificent! How dazzling! How beautiful! So the girl's words were true after all. The embroidery would bring a high price!

Quickly the embroidery was wrapped in clean cloth. Two of the men were sent to Damascus to sell it. "Bring it to the home of the rabbi who lives near the big city," Sarah told them, her eyes flashing. "He often buys such embroideries and will give you a good sum." The men left at once, leaving Sarah with her captors. They rewarded her with a bowl of vegetables and warm rice.

After a few hours the men reached the town and asked where to find the home of the rabbi.

Meanwhile, in the rabbi's house, he and his wife sat and wept. "What could have happened to our beautiful daughter?" they cried. She had often gone to the woods to gather flowers but had always returned. The family, the neighbors, and half of the town had been searching all week for her. But no one had found any trace. At the end of the week, they decided that Sarah must have been attacked by animals in the forest.

Now two men stood at the door, asking to speak to the rabbi. The rabbi invited them to enter and explain the reason for their visit. How surprised he was to see the cloth! Why, there were

Judy Lande Haran

the flowers of the forest, the red, pink, and purple blossoms that his daughter, Sarah, loved so dearly. Between the flowers he recognized the sewn Hebrew letters מ צ ה, with the straight and curved lines around the outside of the design. This was no ordinary cloth! It was a *matzah* cover, which Jews use on *Pesach* to cover their matzot. The rabbi knew at once who had sewn it. His heart beat quickly, but he didn't let his excitement show.

"What fine work!" he said to the two men, as he fingered the embroidery. "I will pay you the sum of twenty gold coins, and I would like to buy two more for the same price, if they can be of the same high quality— and if you can deliver them within one week's time."

The kidnappers could hardly believe their good luck. Why, the picture of the gold coins danced before their eyes. They could hardly wait to return to the cave so that Sarah could begin her work.

For another week Sarah sat, hour after hour, pushing her needle in and out of the cloth, creating designs of beauty. Once again her captors, delighted with the cloth, sent the two men to the rabbi's house to sell it. But this time the rabbi was prepared. He had called the police, who were now watching for the men to return. After the rabbi made his purchase, the police followed the men through the mountains to their hideout in the cave. There they found the rabbi's beautiful daughter, and ten other girls who had been kidnapped, as well. Of course, the girls were quickly freed, and the kidnappers punished.

An embroidered matzah cover made in the U.S.
Leslie Swichkow of Atlanta, Ga.

So it happened that Sarah returned to her family in time for *Pesach*. She and her family celebrated the festival of freedom in great joy. And covering their plate of *matzot* was the beautiful *matzah* cover that Sarah had embroidered and that had saved her life.

CRAFT

An Iron-on Matzah Cover

You can make a *matzah* cover for your own seder. It's easy, but ask an adult to help you if you've never used a hot iron!

WHAT YOU NEED:

fabric crayons
a hot iron
8½" x 11" paper
a large white handkerchief or white cotton fabric, about 14" square

WHAT YOU DO:

1. Draw your design with fabric crayons on the paper. If you use any letters for your design, they will need to be written backwards as if you were looking in a mirror. Use a mirror or window glass to help you. You may draw flowers all around the border and the word מצה or MATZAH in the middle. Or make any pretty design you like.

2. Transfer your fabric crayon design by following the directions below.

3. Heat your iron to HOT (no steam, please, and be careful not to burn your fingers)

4. Place your handkerchief on an ironing board and smooth out all wrinkles.

5. Carefully place your fabric transfer design *face down* onto the handkerchief.

6. Place the iron directly onto the back of the paper. Iron with a short back and forth motion. Continue to iron until you can see the design through the back of the paper. (You can take peeks while you iron, as long as you hold the paper in place.) Remember to turn off the iron when you are done.

7. Gently wash the *matzah* cover in cool water.

What will you write: matzo or matzah?

"Mmm! Nice and crispy!"

RECIPE
Make Your Own Matzah

You may well buy your *matzot* in boxes in the store. But you can also try making your very own *matzot* at home. Here's how. This is the recipe that Barbara's son, David, learned when he was in fourth grade.

WHAT YOU NEED:

2 cups flour
2/3 cup water
mixing bowl
rolling pin
potholder
sheet of wax paper, 12" x 18", to roll the *matzah* on
large flat cookie sheet
fork to make holes in the *matzah*
18 minutes (no more!) for making each *matzah*

WHAT YOU DO:

1. Preheat the oven to 450 degrees Fahrenheit.
2. Measure the flour and water into the mixing bowl, and stir with a fork.
3. Form a small amount of dough into a ball and then use the rolling pin to roll the ball out in a thin, flat circle on wax paper.

Bene Israel men and women in India baking matzah. Script in Hebrew and Marathi.
Poona Haggadah, India, 1874

4. Poke holes in the dough with a fork to keep it from rising.

5. Place the *matzah* on the cookie sheet and, using an oven mitt or potholder, slide it quickly into the oven.

6. Bake the *matzah* for 3–4 minutes, until it is brown. Use the mitt or potholder to remove the cookie sheet from the oven, and don't forget to turn off the oven when you're done.

SEDER TALK

Did Matzah Always Look the Way It Does Now?

The answer is no!

Did you ever wonder why *matzot* have holes? Well, about 1,500 to 1,800 years ago, when the Talmud was written, *matzot* were made with beautiful designs of fish, doves, and flowers stamped on them. But about a thousand years later, the rabbis were afraid that creating the designs might involve handling the *matzah* for more than eighteen minutes, in which time the wheat would leaven and rise.

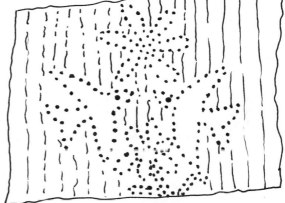

Matzah with designs. Can you find two birds and two flowers?
Lucy Schwartz and Cherie Karo Schwartz

A matzah rake

So the rabbis decided: "From now on no one may make designs on *matzot*." Instead they advised using straight rows of holes. It would be faster, and that way no leavening would take place.

For hundreds of years people used a special little rake for making the holes in the *matzot*.

FUN

Four Matzah Riddles

1. What is whole and full of holes at the same time? Hint: It's crisp and good to eat with *charoset*.

2. What is round and square at the same time?

3. What is the world's largest *matzah*?

4. What is the smallest *matzah*?

Turn the page for the answers

Sue Speier

Is this the way to have matzah on your head? No! It needs to be in a basket!

Riddle answers:

1. A *matzah*, of course!

2. A round plate heaped high with square *matzot*.

3. A *matzah* three feet in diameter. It was made by the Jews in Syria.

4. We are commanded to eat *matzah*, even if it's only the size of an olive. The size has to be enough for a real taste. So, why an olive? Because in ancient Israel olives used to be much larger. One olive was as big as half an egg!

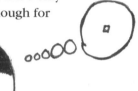

"Hmm . . . an olive . . ."
Seth Rush, age 9

CUSTOMS

Matzah on Your Head

Would you like to sit at the seder table with a basket of *matzot* on your head? Well, during the Middle Ages in Europe, the father would place the three *matzot* in a basket, and place the basket on the head of his son sitting next to him. Some *Haggadot* from the Middle Ages show pictures of boys sitting with the basket of *matzot* on their heads.

Matzah for Everyone

Did you ever hear of *ma'ot chittim* or *ma'os chittim*, which in Hebrew means "money for wheat to bake *matzah*"? This is a special *matzah*-sharing fund that has been going on for hundreds of years, in our country and all over the world.

Here's how it works: Before Passover, the rabbi and a few other people go from house to house to collect money for baking *matzah*. Each person who can afford to make *matzah* must contribute some amount of money to the fund. But people who can't afford to make *matzah* may take money from the fund. Then, hopefully, by the next *Pesach* they'll be able to give money to the fund for others who are in need.

That's a fair way to share. Don't you think so?

PROJECT

How Can You Share Matzah with Others?

In Jewish tradition, when Jews can not bake or buy *matzot*, other Jews send *matzah* to them. Did you know that:

1. During the American Civil War, Union soldiers in the North sent *matzot* to Confederate soldiers in the South to make sure that they could celebrate Passover?
2. The American Joint Distribution Committee is an organization that was started in 1914 to send food (and other help) to Jews all over the world? This is especially important at Passover. Since 1914 the JDC has shipped as many as 70,000 pounds of *matzot* and 20,000 bottles of wine each *Pesach* to Jews in Europe and North Africa.
3. The Jews in Russia have only been able to bake *matzot* or buy them in public for a few years? In the past, Jews in North America, Israel, and other countries sent *matzot* to Russia every year before Passover.

Are there Jews in your community who are too poor to buy *matzot?* How can you help them? Bring boxes of *matzot* to Jewish Family Service, to your congregation, or to your school. The *matzot* will be delivered to families who need them.

MORE CUSTOMS

Four Ways to Break the Middle Matzah

Four customs from around the world:
1. Jews from Morocco break the *matzah* into two parts so the pieces look like the Hebrew letter ה (*heh*) because the letter ה is a symbol for the name of God.
2. Jews of Kurdistan, upon breaking the *matzah* say, "This is the way the Red Sea split for our forefathers."
3. Among Jews from Iraq, Bukhara, and some countries of North Africa:

    Right after the *afikoman* is broken and put away, the *matzot* are shown and the leader says, "This is the bread of affliction, which our forefathers ate in the Land of Egypt." Then one of the

The Hebrew letter heh made from a piece of matzah. Try to do this yourself. Is it easy or hard to do?

"Where have you come from? Where are you going?"

participants quietly leaves the room and ties the two-and-a-half remaining *matzot* in a handkerchief bundle to a stick on his back. After the Four Questions are asked, he enters as a stranger. Then he has a conversation with the participants.

"Where are you from?"

"Egypt."

"Where are you going?"

"To Jerusalem."

"What are you carrying?"

"*Matzot.*"

Then the young people at the seder try to get the *matzah* from the bundle.

Looking for the afikoman.

4. In some Sephardic and Oriental families, the father places the *afikoman* in a bag on his shoulders. Then he carries it around the seder table. Some people believe that when they circle the table they are protecting everyone inside the circle.

Four Ways to Hide the Afikoman

1. In many homes an adult hides the *afikoman*.

2. In some homes the children hide the *afikoman*.

3. In other homes, before the seder starts, several "fake" *afikoman* pieces are hidden around the house. Later, when the search begins, only one of the found pieces will fit back together to form a whole *matzah*. It's like putting together a jigsaw puzzle!

4. At Cherie's seder, her family observes a *minhag* (custom) given to her by her friend, Eliot Spack. Before the seder starts, several "fake" *afikoman* pieces are hidden around the house. Each one is wrapped in a napkin, and each has a small rhyme explaining that it is or isn't the real *afikoman*.

Here are some samples of *afikoman* rhymes that Cherie has created:

- One story leads to another,
  One piece connects to the whole;
  This one's not the *afikoman*,
  Find it elsewhere; that is your goal!

- *Afikoman* low, *afikoman* high:
  You keep looking, and you try;
  Afikoman high, *afikoman* low,
  You have found it. WAY TO GO!

Later, when the search begins, you'll enjoy watching everyone try to find the real *afikoman*.

A NEW CUSTOM

The Matzah of Hope

You can add a fourth *matzah* to the three *matzot* on your plate. This fourth *matzah* is called the "*Matzah* of Hope." While holding it, say a blessing for freedom, like this one, or make up your own: "This is the *Matzah* of Hope for Jews in the world who are not yet free. Next year may they be free to live as Jews in the Land of Israel." This tradition began fairly recently to remind us of the Jews in the former Soviet Union, who were punished for wanting to live as Jews, yet who never gave up hope that one day they could celebrate their religion in freedom.

This special box holds matzot for Pesach. It was created in honor of Israel's 50th birthday celebration.

Judy Lande Haran

At the Seder

*O*nce you've learned about the history of the Jews in Egypt and the crossing to freedom—and once you've cleaned the house, prepared for the seder, and learned about the symbols at the seder table—what else is there to know? Well, as hard as it may be for you to believe, there's still the seder—where we ask yet more questions! And, after the first half of the seder, there is the Festive Meal and the conclusion of the seder. It's a long evening ahead, just as Jewish history is long, and it's a night filled with questions. Before asking "When do we eat?" you might want to turn the page to find out why we ask questions, so many questions, on this night of liberation.

"What flowers should I put on the table?"

INTRODUCTION

Questions are a very important part of Passover: "Why were we slaves in Egypt? Why wouldn't Pharaoh let us leave? How did the sea part?" And, questions are an important part of the seder, too: "Why do we dip vegetables? Why do we recline?" So many questions! Why do we ask questions on Passover? They keep us interested in the story and wanting to know even more about it. But is there another reason? Read this new story about Chelm and decide for yourself.

STORY

Chelm is a small city in Poland. The people who lived there were curious people, always asking questions: "Which is more important, the sun or the moon? How does a child grow: from the feet up or from the head down? How can we keep the sun from disappearing every day?" And the people from Chelm tried to answer the questions in their own "wise" way. When they had a problem that no one could answer, they sought the advice of their village elders—the sages of Chelm—who were the "wisest" of them all.

Passover Clothing in Chelm

A new story about Chelm by Cherie Karo Schwartz and Barbara Rush

Now, the people of Chelm asked questions all year long. But Passover, as you know, is a special time for asking questions. So all of the people of Chelm asked questions about Passover long before Passover began.

Just as Jews everywhere must buy new clothes for *Pesach,* in case a piece of *chametz* might be stuck to the old clothes, the Jews in Chelm wanted to follow this tradition. But how could they possibly carry it out? Why, they barely had enough money to buy soap to wash their old clothing. So they asked each other: "How can we get new clothes for *Pesach?*"

One of the housewives, Mama Perush (**PEHR-oosh**), came up with a perfect solution. "We wear our clothes all year long, and we get used to them. Our neighbors and relatives get used to their clothes, too. But what's old for me can be new for someone else. Yes, women of Chelm,

we must exchange clothes. In that way we will all have something new to wear!"

At once the housewives of Chelm clapped their hands in delight. What a wonderful suggestion! How lucky that Mama Perush had thought of it!

And so, Yente Trina (**YEHN-teh TREE-nah**), the wife of the rabbi, quickly exchanged clothes with Yente Lena (**LEE-nah**), the wife of the *shammes* (**SHAHM-mess**), the one who takes care of the synagogue. Each woman ran home, pleased with her "new" attire.

As soon as she got home, Yente Trina looked in the mirror. Her face turned pale. She gasped in dismay. "Oy! I'm in the wrong house. I thought I was Yente Trina. Now I see that I am Yente Lena." At once she ran out of her house straight for the home of Yente Lena.

Meanwhile Yente Lena, in *her* house, looked in *her* mirror. She too began to gasp. "A disaster! A catastrophe! I thought I was Yente Lena but now I see that I am Yente Trina." And she too left her house and headed straight for the home of Yente Trina.

And what happened? The two women passed each other in the street! They were so upset that they didn't even see each other! Soon, each one arrived at the home of the other. When Yente Trina reached the home of Yente Lena, she began to putter about the kitchen. The *shammes* came home and found the wife of the rabbi in his kitchen. He was quite perplexed. "What are you doing in my house? And where is my wife, Yente Lena?"

Meanwhile Yente Lena, now in the home of Yente Trina, began to clean and tidy up. Later that evening, when the rabbi returned, he was surprised, too. "What are you doing in my house? And where is my wife, Yente Trina?"

It soon became clear that this was a case of mixed-up wives, the first such case in the town of Chelm. There was nothing to do but seek the advice of the sages of Chelm.

The village elders, whose names were Beryl, Shmeryl,

Zak Schwartz, age 17

Yankele, and Yukele, listened to the problem. Each one sighed a deep sigh as each woman told her story.

Yente Trina spoke first: "I exchanged clothes with Yente Lena, and then ran home and looked in the mirror. . . ."

Yente Lena spoke next: "I exchanged clothes with Yente Trina, and then ran home and looked in the mirror. . . ."

At once there was a light upon the face of Beryl the sage. "I have it! I have it!" he cried.

"Tell us, tell us," the two women begged.

"It seems," Beryl said, "that every time you look into the mirror, you turn into someone else."

"Yes," sage Shmeryl continued, "the answer to your problem is this: Each of you must return to your new home and turn the mirrors to the wall. At that moment you will no longer be the new person, but the old person, so you may go back to your old home, and everyone will be as she was before."

Can you imagine how happy this made the women and their husbands? Each woman followed the sage's advice. The moment the mirrors were turned, Yente Trina was no longer Yente Lena, and Yente Lena was no longer Yente Trina. Each woman went back to her own house. And, wonder of wonders, each one was still wearing "new" clothes.

And so, until this very day, the people of Chelm practice the custom of exchanging clothes—as well as turning the mirrors to the wall—during Passover. In fact, not only the women, but also the men and children, exchange clothes. True, this causes a bit of an inconvenience every year, but the Chelmites do not mind. "After all," they ask, "isn't it according to tradition to have 'new' clothes for the holiday?"

CUSTOMS

May You Live to 120!
סד ביסת סללה בראסיד

How do we greet each other at Passover? May you live to 120! This greeting, which Jews from Persia say to each other at their seders, looks like Hebrew, doesn't it? That's because it's written in Hebrew letters. But it isn't Hebrew. It is a language that combines Hebrew and Persian and is called Judeo-Persian.

The words say: "*Sahd, Bist, Sah-leh, Berasid.*" They mean: May you live to be 120 years old! It's a greeting that many Jews use to wish each other happy birthday.

Now what does this birthday greeting have to do with Passover? Well, according to the Bible, Passover is the beginning of the year. So, the seder is a kind of birthday party for the year and for all the people at the seder. That is why Jews from Persia wish each other birthday greetings on Passover. Why wish for a life of 120 years? Because that's the same number of birthdays that Moses celebrated.

New Clothing for Passover

Why do people wear new clothing for Passover?

Remember that Jews are required at Passover to eliminate all of their *chametz,* leavened foods, from their homes. Since crumbs could easily get lost in the pockets of clothes, people used to buy a new outfit—or have clothes made—for the holiday. This might be their one new outfit for the whole year!

If people could not afford new clothes, then their old clothes were washed especially carefully.

What are you going to wear to the Passover seder?

There are many different customs about what to wear to the seder. Some people buy new clothes. Moroccans, Yemenites, and Samaritans wear loose-fitting white robes, and Moroccan women wear white scarves on their heads since white is a symbol of freedom.

The Jews of Bukhara wear bright-colored, beautiful gowns, red scarves, and lots of gold jewelry, perhaps because, according to the Torah (Exodus 3:22), the Jewish women took gold jewelry with them as they left *Mitzrayim!*

Men from Kurdistan wear *keffiyahs* (**kehf-FEE-yahs**), long scarf-type head coverings wrapped around their heads.

"Secret Jews" in Spain and Portugal at the end of the fifteenth century wore traveling clothes and carried walking sticks, as if they were going on a journey into the desert, seeking freedom. Jews in Portugal today, whose families were once "secret Jews," still dress this way at the seder.

Passover clothing from Morocco.
Simha Shemesh

WHY DOES THE TALMUD TELL US THAT THE ONE WHO ASKS THE QUESTIONS SHOULD BE GIVEN NUTS TO EAT? MAYBE BECAUSE THE ASKER "CRACKED THE SHELL" TO FIND THE RIGHT ANSWER!

"What should I wear to the seder?"

FUN

Something New for Your Seder

Spring and Passover are times for new beginnings. Can you think of something new to do for your seder this year? Will this be the year that you ask the Four Questions? Or will you read part of the *Haggadah* in Hebrew? *B'hatzlacha!* (**B'hahtz-lah-CHAH!**) In Hebrew that means "May you succeed!" Lots of luck on your new adventure.

THE FOUR QUESTIONS

Why Is This Night Different?

Are you prepared to ask the Four Questions at your seder? Have you studied the questions in English, and practiced reciting them in Hebrew? Do you know the melody? If you're like many other children who ask the questions each year, your palms will sweat until it's over—and you can sit and listen to the answer. Don't worry about making a mistake. Everyone at the table is cheering for you. Just relax, and know that you are connecting the past and the future in Jewish tradition.

The Four Questions form an important part of the seder because parents and children each participate in this section. In many homes, the youngest child at the seder asks the Four Questions.

"Why is this night different from all other nights? (*Mah nishtahnah ha'lailah hazeh?*)"

1. Why do we eat only unleavened bread on Passover?

2. Why do we eat bitter herbs on Passover?

3. Why do we dip vegetables twice on Passover?

4. Why do we recline at the Passover seder table?

The Four Questions in German.
Geismar Haggadah, Germany, 1928

Did you know that the Four Questions were not always asked by the youngest child? That custom was only started in Eastern Europe in the seventeenth century! In some places in Morocco, everyone at the seder asked the Four Questions together in one loud voice. In Djerba, in North Africa, the father asked the questions, and the youngest child answered them!

Did you know that at one time the Four Questions were asked at the end of the seder? Long ago the questions were actually statements: "How different this night is! How we dip twice!" And these statements were made at the end of the seder. But then people noticed that the children were falling asleep before the end. So, they moved the statements to the beginning of the seder and changed them into the Four Questions.

The first letter of "Mah Nishtahnah."
Livorno Haggadah, Italy, 1867

MORE CUSTOMS

What Are Some Different Ways to Ask the Four Questions?

With your family and friends, create new questions—besides the Four Questions—to ask at the seder. Here are some ideas (or create your own questions) about community, the world, peace, and other subjects:

Why is this seder different from all other seders?

1. What are some things that have been new for each of us this past year?
2. Where have we been on our journeys and travels in the past year?
3. What are some things that were new in the Jewish world this past year?
4. What are some ways that we have made our seder new this year?

Here's yet another question: "How is our family different from all other families?"

And, "How is our family the same as all other families?"

Judy Lande Haran

SONG

Here are two melodies for asking the Four Questions.

Mah Nishtanah

Traditional

Mah nish-ta-nah ha - lai - lah ha-ze mi - kol___ ha - lei -
lot mi - kol___ ha - lei - lot she-b'- chol ha-lei - lot
a - nu okh - lin cha - metz___ u - ma - tzah cha -
metz___ u - ma - tzah ha - lai - lah ha-ze ha -
lai - lah ha - zeh ku - lo___ ma - tzah___ ha - tzah

Why is this night different from all other nights?
On all other nights we eat either chametz or
matzah.
Why, on this night, do we eat only matzah?

מַה נִּשְׁתַּנָּה הַלַּיְלָה הַזֶּה מִכָּל הַלֵּילוֹת.

שֶׁבְּכָל הַלֵּילוֹת אָנוּ אוֹכְלִין חָמֵץ וּמַצָּה,
הַלַּיְלָה הַזֶּה כֻּלּוֹ מַצָּה.

Mah Nishtanah

*Repeat in similar fashion
for additional verses*

Why is this night different from all other nights?
On this night why do we eat matza and bitter herbs;
dip parsley in salt water and horseradish in charoset;
and why do we recline at the table when we eat?

מַה נִּשְׁתַּנָּה הַלַּיְלָה הַזֶּה מִכָּל הַלֵּילוֹת.
שֶׁבְּכָל הַלֵּילוֹת אָנוּ אוֹכְלִין חָמֵץ וּמַצָּה
הַלַּיְלָה הַזֶּה כֻּלּוֹ מַצָּה.

SEDER TALK

How Have the Four Questions Changed Over the Years?

Many years ago, the fourth question was: Why do we roast lamb meat for Passover? After the Jews returned to the Holy Land from Egypt, and after the Holy Temple was built in Jerusalem, families from all over the country would go to Jerusalem on *Pesach*. At the Holy Temple they would roast a lamb and eat a *Pesach* feast. But after the Temple was destroyed, the Jewish people went to many different lands. They no longer went to Jerusalem to sacrifice the lambs. So the question about roasting the meat was no longer necessary. Instead, the fourth question was changed to: "On this night, why do we recline?"

CRAFT

The "Four Questions" Kippah

Many Jews wear a head covering all the time. Others wear a head covering only while praying or when in synagogue or temple. You can create a special *kippah* (**kee-PAH**, also known as a *yarmulke*) for the person (boy or girl) who recites the Four Questions at your seder. Buy a plain *kippah* in any color. Use fabric paints to divide the *kippah* into four sections. Draw a big question mark or many smaller question marks in each section. Print, in Hebrew or English, the first words from the Four Questions around the bottom edge of the *kippah*. ("Why is this night different?"; *"Mah nish tah nah ha'lailah hazeh?"*)

Zak Schwartz, age 17

This will be your special "Four Questions" *kippah* every year at your seder. Whoever recites the Four Questions may wear the special cap. You now have a *new* family tradition!

MORE FUN

Find Other "Fours" in the Seder

Pretend that you are a *seder* detective! How many fours can you find in the *Haggadah?* Give yourself four points for each right answer. Here are some clues:

What are the four of these that we drink?

What are the four of these that we ask?

What are the four of these children?

What are the four of these that we crunch?

EXTRA HARD QUESTIONS: Give yourself ten points for each of these!

What are two sets of four of these that we sing at the seder?

What are four ways that God told the Children of Israel they would be saved?

What are four ways to welcome Elijah (**Ee-LYE-jah**) the Prophet?

What is another four that we haven't asked yet?

What is your score?

Are you a super detective? Can you think of any other fours in Judaism?

(CLUE: How many tens of years did the Israelites wander in the desert?)

Coby Gould, age 12

Be a Seder Detective

Can you answer this: How do you know that Lot celebrated Passover?

Look in the Torah in Genesis 19.

Here is a clue. Look for these words: "unleavened bread."

Did you find it yet? No? Here's another clue:

Look for this word: "feast."

Are you wondering how Lot could have celebrated *Pesach* if the Jews hadn't even gone to Egypt? Good question!

MORE SEDER TALK

The Four Sons

Another part of the seder has four questions. Can you find it? Remember the Four Sons—one wise, one wicked, one simple, and one who does not know how to ask? The *Haggadah* tells us that each son asks a question and suggests how we should answer each child. Can you think of new ways to answer these old questions? Can you think of new questions, such as:

1. What can we say to Wise Children to make them want to know even more?
2. What can we say to Wicked Children to make them want to reconnect with others and their own tradition?
3. What can we say to Simple Children so that they will understand more?
4. What can we say to Shy Children so that they will be able to ask questions?

The Four Sons in a very old and rare Haggadah from Czechoslovakia.
Prague Haggadah, Czechoslovakia, 1777.

How Are We Like the Four Sons?

How is each one of us like all four of the children?

We are like the wise son when we are very smart. We have learned well!

We are like the wicked son when we do not acknowledge that we belong with our own tradition.

We are like the simple son when we do not understand everything that happens.

We are like the son not able to ask when we do not know enough to ask why.

YET ANOTHER CUSTOM

Four or Five Cups of Wine?

How many cups of wine do we drink at the seder . . . four or five?

At the seder, each person drinks four cups of wine. Why four? Because the Torah tells us of four ways that God freed the Children of Israel from slavery in Egypt:

"I will free you from the slavery of Egypt."

"I will deliver you from their slavery."

"I will redeem you with an outstretched arm."

"I will take you to be My people."

At some seders, some families add a fifth cup of wine to remember the promise in the Torah: "I will bring you into the Land." They drink the fifth cup of wine to show their gratitude for the State of Israel, where all Jews may live in freedom.

INTRODUCTION

"Dayenu" (**dye-EH-noo**) is one of the seder's best-loved songs, the one most people remember long after the last cup is emptied and the seder ends. At many seders, everyone sings the song together. In some homes, one person sings the verses, and everyone else sings "Dayenu!" together, then joins in the chorus. Cherie's family has a contest to see who can sing the verses fastest!

What does Dayenu really mean?

The word dayenu is the Hebrew for "it would have been enough" or "we would have been satisfied." The song is actually a story about all the miracles that God performed for the Jewish people to free us from Mitzrayim. Our enemies were punished; we crossed the sea on dry land; we received the Torah; we were brought into Israel; and we built the Holy Temple. It is a song about being grateful, and it tells the story one step at a time. At each step of the way, we say "dayenu" ("it would have been enough").

But, when is enough? We always seem to want more of everything—more toys, more dessert, more things. This song tells us that we should be thankful for all that we do have; we should be satisfied one step at a time, and at every step, we should give thanks.

> **DAYENU:** WHAT WONDERFUL THINGS GOD HAS DONE FOR US! HOW ABUNDANT ARE ALL OF GOD'S BLESSINGS.

STORY

This story has been told in many places: Eastern Europe, Yemen, Syria, Turkey, Tunisia. To write this version, we combined a story from Tunisia in North Africa with a story from Galicia (a part of Poland) in Eastern Europe. The melody was sung by Jews in Galicia.

Dayenu

a folktale retold by Barbara Rush

In the faraway land of Galicia in Poland, a king owned a beautiful ring made of pure gold. It was set with diamonds, rubies, and other precious jewels. In all the world no ring was as costly or glittered as brightly as this one! But just four days before *Pesach* the king's ring was stolen!

Now, the king's advisor, whose name was Dayenu, hated the Jews.

"Your Majesty, do you know who has stolen your precious ring?"

Larry Schwartz

Dayenu asked the king. "The Jews! And why? Because they have a holiday that is coming very soon, a holiday called *Pesach*. The Jews need a lot of money for this holiday, and they plan to sell your ring to get the money."

When the king heard these words, his eyes narrowed in anger. At once he issued a decree: "If my ring is not returned in ten days, all the Jews will be killed!"

The Jews were terrified. How well they knew that none of them had stolen the ring! But how could they prove their innocence?

Now, among the community of Jews was a poor man named Beryl (**BEH-rill**). His children went barefoot. His family was hungry. With *Pesach* approaching, he did not have money for a seder. Beryl was desperate. So he went to the king's palace and asked to see the king. "Your Majesty, why have you issued this terrible decree?" he asked.

"Because someone stole my ring," the king replied.

"Permit me to tell you, Your Majesty, only one person committed this theft. Do you think it is fair to kill thousands of people for the crime of one person?"

The king grew curious. "How do you know it was only one person? Do you know the name of the thief?"

Beryl thought about this. Here was his chance to get what he needed for *Pesach*. "Yes, I can identify him. That is why I have come here. But only if you fill my request will I tell you his name."

"Very well," said the king. "I will give you what you ask for, but you must tell me the thief's name."

"I would like twenty boxes of *matzos,*" Beryl answered, "twenty bottles of wine, two sheep, clothes for my family, and a thousand coins besides. Then, after the holiday of *Pesach,* I will tell you who the thief is."

The king thought to himself, "What! How dare this poor Jew make demands on me, the king!" The truth is that the king wanted to kill the Jew for being so bold. But he also wanted to learn the identity of the thief. He knew that if he did not do as Beryl asked, he might never solve his problem. So he called to his advisor. "Give the Jew what he wants. After *Pesach,* if he does not tell us what we want to know, he and all his people will be executed."

So Beryl returned home, his arms heaped high with food for the seder, his pockets jingling with the sound of coins.

Lucy Schwartz, age 15

But do you think the king was so foolish as to let Beryl go home with all that money without having him followed? Of course not! He called his palace guards and sent three of them to watch Beryl day and night as he and his family prepared for the seder. Days passed. On the eve of Passover, Beryl began to read the *Haggadah*. "Let all who are hungry come and eat!" he called out.

The guards heard Beryl's words. As they were very hungry, they entered the house and sat at the table. How better to keep an eye on Beryl? So, they watched as Beryl broke a strange flat bread in half and spread strange, muddy-looking food on it. They listened as melodies were sung in a language they could not understand. Beryl was singing, *"Ilu-hoytsi-onu mi Mitsrayim . . ."* ("If He saved us from Egypt . . .") And everyone at the table sang in answer, *"Da-ye-nu!"* ("It would have been enough!")

The guards could not believe their ears. Why would the family be calling out Dayenu, the name of the king's advisor?

Again Beryl sang, *"Ilu nosan lonu es ha Toyre . . ."* ("If He had given us the Torah . . . ") And again the family answered all together, *"Da-ye-nu!"* ("It would have been enough!")

The song continued. Over and over the name of the king's advisor was repeated. The guards were amazed. Everyone was singing the name of Dayenu, the king's advisor. But why?

As soon as the seder was over, the guards ran as quickly as they could to the palace, and reported these strange happenings to the king, even though it was the middle of the night.

The king listened. "The Jews' words could have only one meaning," he declared. "Dayenu, my trusted advisor, must be the thief!"

That very morning the king's guards searched the home of Dayenu. There, hidden in a silver box, they found the ring!

Then the guards went to Beryl's house and knocked at the door. When Beryl saw the guards, he grew frightened. "What do you want?" he asked.

"The king wishes to see you."

"Oh, no!" Beryl thought. "The king told me I had ten days to tell him who the thief is. But I don't know who it is yet. What shall I do?"

In a trembling voice, Beryl answered, "Tell the king that today I am busy. Only after my holiday will I tell him the thief's name."

To this the guards replied, "Oh, the king already knows the identity of the thief. Last night we heard you call out the name, Dayenu, and we went to inform the king of our discovery. And, indeed, it was in Dayenu's house that we found the ring. You can be sure that Dayenu has been thrown in prison."

After hearing these words, Beryl finally understood what had happened. He chuckled to himself and said a prayer of thanks. Then his voice grew bold: "It was not by accident that I called out Dayenu in a loud voice, for I knew that you, the king's guards, were seated at my table, and I wanted you to hear my words and keep them on your lips when you reported to the king."

And so the Jew returned to the palace with the guards.

The king happily embraced the poor man. "You shall be the head of all the Jews in my kingdom," he announced. And then the king called for every one of his ministers to bring a present for the Jew.

But Beryl bowed his head. "You must forgive me, Your Majesty," he said, "but today is a holiday for the Jews, and we are forbidden to take money. If I go against the law of my religion, it will be as if I accepted another religion. Perhaps you will allow me to return another day to accept your generous gifts."

"Ah," cried the king, "in all my kingdom I will not find a man as faithful as you. Go in peace to celebrate your holiday."

After that, Beryl and his family—and all the Jews of the country—lived in peace and happiness. And every year, just before *Pesach,* the Jews received a large gift of money from the king so that even the poorest Jew could celebrate the holiday in peace and in blessing.

Why do you think it was so important for Jews in many different places to tell this story? To answer this question, remember that most of these stories were told when Jews came to Israel in the early 1950s, just after the State of Israel was established as a safe home for all Jews. Many of these Jews had just escaped from the Holocaust; others had come from countries where they were not free to live as Jews. So, a story about being saved might have had special meaning for these people.

Also remember that many folktales are stories of wishes that come true. This means that sometimes you do not get your wish in real life but your wish can come true in a story.

SONG

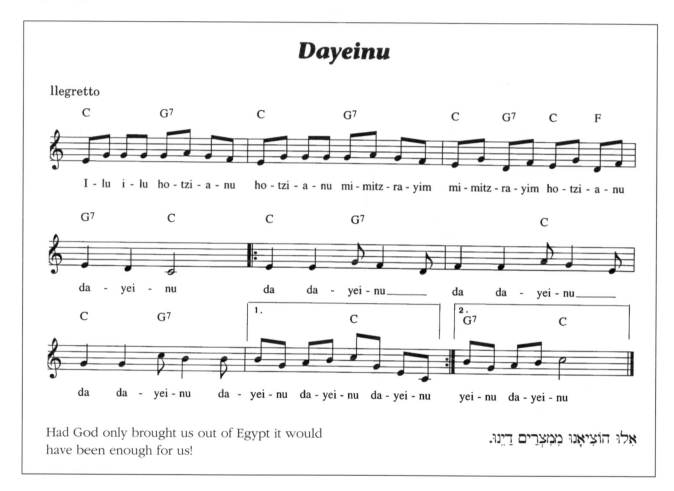

Dayeinu

llegretto

I - lu i - lu ho - tzi - a - nu ho - tzi - a - nu mi - mitz - ra - yim mi - mitz - ra - yim ho - tzi - a - nu

da - yei - nu da da - yei - nu_____ da da - yei - nu_____

da da - yei - nu da - yei - nu da - yei - nu da - yei - nu yei - nu da - yei - nu

Had God only brought us out of Egypt it would have been enough for us!

אִלּוּ הוֹצִיאָנוּ מִמִּצְרַיִם דַּיֵּנוּ.

Here are all the verses of "*Dayenu*" put together:

"How thankful we are for the many good things God has given to us: If God freed us from Egypt, destroyed their idols, brought judgment on them, gave us their wealth, parted the sea for us, brought us across on dry land, drowned our enemies, kept us alive in the wilderness forty years, fed us manna, gave us the Sabbath, brought us to Mount Sinai, gave us the Torah, brought us into the Land of Israel, and built the Holy Temple. *Dayenu!* How abundant are all of God's blessings!"

FUN

A New "Dayenu"

Create your own version of *"Dayenu"* for yourself, your family, or your community seder. Maybe you will want to ask, "Would it have been enough?" Here's an example for you:

If I had been born, but didn't have anyone to take care of me, would it have been enough?

If I had someone to take care of me, but didn't have anyone to feed me, would it have been enough?

If I had someone to feed me, but didn't have anyone to play with me, would it have been enough?

If I had someone to play with me, but didn't have anyone to read to me, would it have been enough?

If I had someone to read to me, but didn't have anyone to teach me, would it have been enough?

If I had someone to teach me, but didn't have anyone to love me, is this ever enough?

Question:

Can you think of some other ideas for a new *"Dayenu"*? How about one for taking care of the world or making peace with each other?

And Another "Dayenu"

Some people have added a new kind of *Dayenu* to their seder: "It was not enough" (*Lo Dayenu*). Here are a few examples:

If we see someone hurting, but do not try to help, *Lo Dayenu!*

If we see hunger in the world, but do not help feed others, *Lo Dayenu!*

If we give the same love and respect to some people, but not all people, *Lo Dayenu!*

If we see a chance to do a *mitzvah* (a good deed) and do not do it, *Lo Dayenu!*

Larry and Cherie Schwartz

CRAFT
A Micrography Picture

A micrography picture is a drawing made with alphabet letters instead of with solid lines!

Micrography may look like a big word, but look at it closely. It sounds like the word microscope, which means seeing little things. So micrography means writing little letters.

Micrography is an ancient Jewish art. It was made popular years ago by artists living in the city of Tzfat (Safed) in Israel. Micrography is still being made today. You can make your own micrography art by using tiny letters and words to create shapes so that the picture represents what the words say and mean.

At the Passover seder, we sing many Psalms of thanks to God. For example, the words from Psalm 136 are found in the *Haggadah:* "Praise God for God is good . . . who . . . brought out Israel from among them with a strong hand and an outstretched arm." You could write these words into the shape of an arm . . . or a hand or a wave in the sea!

Create a special micrography picture to hang at your seder. It's actually very easy to do.

WHAT YOU NEED:

Colored pencils, pens, or fine-tip magic markers
scrap paper for practicing
large light-colored paper (white, yellow, pale blue) the size you
    would like your picture to be

WHAT YOU DO:

1. Write a prayer of thanks to God in Hebrew or English. It can be one or more sentences.
2. Choose a shape that you want to make into a micrography picture. It can be a Passover symbol like *matzah,* the Cup of Elijah, spring flowers, or symbols on the seder plate. Or if you choose a prayer that has a special subject, like peace or hope, draw a shape that represents the theme. (For peace, you could make the shape of a dove.)
3. For practice, draw the shape with pencil on a piece of scrap paper, and then write the sentence and words in very small letters around the drawn line. You may want to include Hebrew words as well as

Barbara Rush

English. See how they form the shape? Do you have to write them more than one time around the shape? Do you want to add more words or sentences to fill in the space of the shape?

4. After you have practiced, draw the shape and letters with pencil on the good paper, and color it lightly so you will still see the words.

Let your imagination soar! Create a special micrography picture that can be used for years to come.

CUSTOM

A Persian Scallion "Battle"

Barbara's friend, Azariah Levy, whose family came to Israel from Persia (Iran), shared this custom with us. Jews from Persia have a special seder custom at the time of reciting and singing "*Dayenu.*" When they say, "Had God taken us out of Egypt . . . ," everyone at the table picks up the scallions from the seder plate. When they say the word "*Dayenu,*" they hit each other lightly on the back or shoulders with the scallions to remind themselves of how it felt to be slaves.

Barbara Rush

"Dayenu!"

"We're having a scallion battle!"

INTRODUCTION

Now that you've told the Exodus story, recited the blessings, and explained the meaning of the symbols on the seder plate, it's finally time to eat the festive meal! Close your Haggadot *and relax. Now you can feast on the delicious food of the Passover meal before you complete the rest of the seder.*

What foods do you think most people eat on Passover? Matzah? Right! Jews all over the world eat matzot, *but not all* matzot *are the same size or shape. Matzah can be thick or thin, round or square, flat or fluffy. The Karaites (Jews who follow the laws of the Bible but do not accept the later teaching of the Rabbis) ate* matzot *made from barley, not from wheat. Some Jews will eat* matzot, *but refuse to eat anything made with* matzot, *like* matzah *balls or* matzah *pudding.*

Matzah balls? Not all Jews eat them, believe it or not. Matzah balls are eaten mostly by Jews whose families came from Eastern Europe, where matzah *balls were—and still are—a traditional food prepared for the seder. Most* matzah *balls are spiced with a bit of salt and pepper, but some Jews in Louisiana make them with gumbo spice, a "hot" flavoring used in the southern part of the United States.*

"We're ready to cook . . ."

What about rice? Did you know that some Jews (from Ashkenazic backgrounds) think rice is forbidden, while other Jews (from Sephardic backgrounds) purposely do eat rice because they believe that the many grains of rice will bring them good luck?

By now you've figured out that not all Jews eat the same foods at their seders. What you eat depends on where your family lived hundreds of years ago, where you live now, and what your family likes to eat. So, get ready for some great food! But

". . . and set the table."

first, just as at your seder table, here's a story before the food is brought in from the kitchen.

STORY

Hershele Ostropoler (**HER-shell-eh OS-troh-poh-lehr**), or just plain Hershele as he was known by his neighbors, was a very clever man who lived in Poland about two hundred years ago. He was very poor, but he usually got enough to eat by using his wit. The stories of Hershele's many adventures are so delightful that they are still told around the world today. This is our Passover version of one of the Hershele stories.

Hershele's Passover Feast

A new story about Hershele by Cherie Karo Schwartz and Barbara Rush

Once, during Passover, Hershele decided to take a walk. It was a warm day. After the hard, cold winter, it felt so grand to walk in the fresh air and see the trees and plants and grass coming back to life. Even the birds were happy, and they kept Hershele company with their singing. Hershele was having such a wonderful time walking that he didn't notice where he was going. Suddenly, he found himself in the middle of the forest. He was hopelessly lost . . . and very hungry! (For even though Hershele had eaten well at the seder, his stomach was empty again, as usual!)

Elana Blumenfeld-Gantz, age 10

"Oy, I am so hungry that I can hear my tummy rumbling! Oy, I am so hungry that I can barely stand up! Oy, I am so hungry that I think I'm going to faint!" said Hershele to the birds and the trees and the sky. "But, wait a minute! I almost forgot who I am. I am Hershele Ostropoler. I come from a long line of people who know how to get what they want. I will get a good snack! Even better, I will get a *great* meal!"

Hershele was proud of himself for coming up with such a wonderful thought, but he still had no idea where to find such a meal. After all, as his father had always told him, "Chickens don't grow on trees!"

"Too bad," thought Hershele. "There are certainly lots of trees around here."

Hershele made his way to a clearing, and what did he see? Across the meadow was a little hut. Coming out of the chimney was a trail of smoke. "Hoo hah! There's someone home. And since it's far too warm to have a fire in the house, I'll bet that someone is cooking. And since it's early in the day, I'll bet that it's someone Jewish making more delicious foods for Passover. What will it be this time? Borscht, a delicious beet soup? *Matzo kugel*, a nice *matzo* pudding? Roasted potatoes? Yum!"

Hershele could hardly move his feet fast enough. He practically ran to the little hut and banged on the door. In his sweetest voice he called out, "Yoo hoo! Anybody home?"

Not a sound came from inside the house. So he tried knocking again. "It's me, Hershele Ostropoler! I've come for a Passover visit!"

The door remained closed, but Hershele heard a voice inside: "I don't know who you are, and I don't want any visitors."

"Hmm," thought Hershele, "this calls for serious measures." "Oh, that's all right," he answered. "You must have had many guests for your seder, and now you're tired. I understand. Maybe you haven't had time to clean the house yet. I'll tell you what. You can just open the door and offer me something to eat. I won't bother you."

There was a pause. Then the voice inside the hut said, "Please go away. I don't have any food."

Hershele looked up at the chimney. He saw the smoke. He smelled the food. Ah, he could almost taste it! He had to have something to eat. "Kind woman, you must give me something to eat. I must have some food right away."

Elana Blumenfeld-Gantz, age 10

GO AWAY!

"No, I have nothing. Please go away!"

Hershele thought for a minute. Then he cried out in a deep, loud voice: "If you don't give me something to eat right now, I will have to do what my father did!"

Inside the hut, the woman was thinking, "What did his father do? Who was his father? Maybe he was a mean man, or a man with a terrible temper . . . or maybe he was even a robber! Oy! Oy! Whatever am I to do?" Quickly, she gathered up some of the leftovers from her seder dinner, put them into a basket, and set the basket outside the door. Then she shut the door fast. Whew!

Outside, Hershele opened the basket and took a deep breath. He sat on a rock and smelled all the good foods. "That's more like it! Thank you, kind woman." And with that he ate up the leftover seder foods, and even a bit of chopped *charoses*. He smacked his lips after the delicious meal, but a few moments later felt hungry again. He smelled something wonderful cooking on the stove. Unable to contain himself, he called, "I'd really like you to bring me some more food, or I might have to do what my father did!"

For a few moments there was silence. Inside the house the woman thought, "What did his father do? What did his father do? It must have been something terrible." So, once again she opened the door. This time she set out a plate of *matzos*.

"Not bad," thought Hershele as he gobbled up every crumb.

But the smells of wonderful cooking still drifted toward Hershele's nose. He knew that there was still good food inside the house.

So, for a third time, he called, "Thank you, good woman, but I'd like you to bring me just a bit more food. If not, I might have to do what my father did."

This time the woman was a bit more frightened, and a bit more curious.

Soon, hustling and bustling sounds could be heard inside the house. Then the door was flung open, and the woman handed Hershele a huge bowl of steaming soup with fluffy *matzo* balls floating on top. A moment later she disappeared into the house. Hershele sat down on his rock again. He noisily slurped the soup, and finished all the *matzo* balls, as well.

At last, Hershele leaned back and patted his stuffed belly. He gave a big satisfied burp, and carefully wiped his chin on his shirtsleeve. Then, with a big yawn, he got up and called out, "Thank you, kind woman, for the delicious food. I haven't had such a feast since *Purim*. Goodbye!" And Hershele started to head off down the road.

As Hershele was leaving, the door of the hut opened, and the woman poked her head out. "Excuse me, stranger," she called. "I've given you all the food in my house. The least you can do is answer one question."

Hershele stopped and turned around. "Gladly," he said. "What is it that you want to know?"

"Well, what were you going to do if I didn't give you any food? What did your father do?"

Hershele turned around and began walking down the road. When he was almost out of sight, he turned back toward the hut and called out, "When my father couldn't get anything to eat . . . he went hungry!"

And that is a story of Hershele Ostropoler!

CUSTOMS

What Do Jews Eat at Their Seders?

Ashkenazic Jews eat foods like:

* *tsimmes,* a stew of fruits and vegetables, and sometimes meat.

Cherie's family makes *tsimmes* with potatoes, onions, carrots, parsley, and lots of garlic, boiled and then mashed together. Barbara's family uses peeled potatoes, meat, and prunes, baked for hours until the potatoes turn brown;

* *knaidlach* (**KNAY-dlach** in Yiddish), *matzo* balls for soup, made from ground *matzo* (called *matzo* meal) and eggs, oil, water, and spices, formed into balls and cooked in liquid;

* *compote,* a variety of dried fruits, cooked together into a fruit stew;

* *gefilte fish,* ground fish boiled with onions and carrots and spices;

* *matzo farfel kugel,* a pudding made from crumbled *matzo* (called *matzo farfel*), baked with water and beaten eggs. This is such a favorite that when President Clinton became president, the staff at the White House made a seder, and guess what they served? You guessed it! *Matzo farfel kugel!*

Cherie's family likes their kugel with fried onions and spices. Barbara's family eats a sweeter kugel, made with apricots, sugar, and cinnamon.

Ashkenazic Jews do *not* eat rice or corn, beans or lentils because these can be ground into flour for making *chametz*. Most Ashkenazic Jews do not eat lamb on Passover because it is a reminder of the days when lambs were sacrificed at the Holy Temple.

ASHKENAZIC RECIPE

Knaidlach or Matzo Balls

Matzo balls are usually eaten with chicken soup at the early part of the meal. Everyone has a different idea of what perfect *matzo* balls (*knaidlach*) look and taste like.

"Just the way I like them!"

WHAT IS THE PERFECT
PASSOVER MATZO BALL
QUESTION?
I KNOW: "FLUFFY OR HARD?"

Because this recipe calls for boiling water, be sure to get an adult
to help you.

This recipe will make about twenty *matzo* balls.

WHAT YOU NEED:

6 large eggs
2 cups vegetable shortening
3/4 cup chicken broth or water
2 tablespoons parsley flakes
2 teaspoons salt (only if you are using water instead of chicken
    broth)
pepper (optional)
1 cup *matzo* meal
medium-size mixing bowl
fork for mixing
8-quart stock pot
large, long-handled soup
    spoon
wax paper
plastic wrap

WHAT YOU DO:

1. Break the eggs into the mixing bowl. Be careful not to let
the eggshells fall into the
bowl. Beat the eggs with the
fork.

2. Add the shortening and continue beating until blended.

3. Add the water or chicken
broth, parsley flakes, salt, and pepper.

4. Stir the ingredients well.

5. Add the *matzo* meal and stir.

6. Cover the mixing bowl with plastic wrap and place it in the refrigerator for at least two hours.

7. When the 2 hours are up, put 6 quarts of water into the stock pot
and heat it on the stove until it boils. (Putting a lid on the pot will
help the water heat more quickly.)

8. While the water is heating up, roll one tablespoon of mix at a time
in your hands to form round *matzo* balls. Keep rolling until you

Making the perfect matzo balls.

have used up all of the batter. Arrange the balls in a single layer on wax paper and don't let them touch (they will stick together).

HINT: If your hands get sticky while you're forming the balls, wet your hands under running water. This will keep the mixture from sticking to your hands.

9. Use a long-handled spoon to place the *matzo* balls (carefully!) into the boiling water. Boil for twenty minutes.

CUSTOMS

Floaters or Sinkers?

Barbara's family loves fluffy *matzo* balls. In her family it's considered a disgrace (a *shanda,* in Yiddish) to serve *matzo* balls that are hard. Barbara says: "My Aunt Judith made the fluffiest *matzo* balls I ever saw. Each one was the size of a large orange. To get the *knaidlach* so fluffy, she beat the egg whites separately until they stood up, then she added the beaten egg white mixture

Soup's on! Get it while it's hot!
Lucy Wohlauer, age 12

to the *matzo* meal mixture. She cooked them in the soup *for several hours* until all the water was absorbed into the *knaidlach*. She made an extra pot of soup for eating with the *matzo* balls." But some families prefer harder *matzo* balls. If you want harder *matzo* balls, add a tiny bit more *matzo* meal to the recipe.

Cherie's and Barbara's friend, Peninnah Schram, remembers her mother making the special *matzo* balls that her grandmother had made in Lithuania: with an egg yolk in the middle! Can you guess how she did it? Clue: The yolk must be hard before the *matzo* ball is formed. The answer is printed in the margin.

Other *matzo* meal hints:

1. Some people use club soda instead of water to make extra-fluffy *matzo* balls!
2. Cherie's friends, Rabbi Zalman Schachter-Shalomi and his wife, Eve Ilsen, add caraway seeds.
3. German Jews add spicy red pepper.

ANSWER: Hard boil an egg ahead of time. When cool, remove the shell and the white (you can eat the cooked white). Be careful not to break the cooked yolk. When forming *matzo* balls (as in the last recipe), roll some batter around the cooked yolk. Cook this special *matzo* ball with the others.

4. Are there any seder guests who need to be careful of their cholesterol level? Then use only the egg whites, and beat them until they're fluffy.

> Can you imagine *matzo* balls that are as small as buttons? Barbara's friend, Simone Lipman, says that when she was a child, Jews in France and Germany made tiny *matzo* balls, which they called "*matzo* buttons." The children had fun making dozens and dozens of them for Passover.

Favorite Sephardic Seder Foods

Sephardic and Oriental Jews may eat some of these foods at their seders:

- *fruits and vegetables,* such as artichokes, carrots, beets, olives, leeks, spinach, and eggplant, that grow in countries like Greece, Italy, Morocco, Algiers, Iraq, Iran, Yemen, and other countries in Asia, Africa, and southern Europe.
- *soups and other foods* made with beans and rice;
- *frittata,* a vegetable and egg pie made with *matzah* and leeks, spinach, or Swiss chard. These are served as an appetizer at the *seder;*
- *mina,* a kind of layered pie, made with layers of *matzah,* with meat and veggies in between;
- *caponata,* a spicy eggplant stew, made with olives, peppers, onions, and spices, which is eaten cold;
- *pastelicos,* fried mashed potato balls with meat inside;
- *bimuelos, matzah* cupcakes or doughnuts.

SEPHARDIC RECIPES

Italian Rice Soup

Italian Jews love to eat this delicious, simple-to-make soup on *Pesach.* (Remember that Sephardic Jews may eat rice and beans on *Pesach.*) The many grains of rice serve as a symbol of all the good things that will happen in the new season. The egg is a symbol of new life in the spring. This is our simple-to-make version of this soup.

This recipe calls for boiling water, so please ask an adult to help you. And here's a hint: You can cook the rice and eggs in advance. This recipe makes six to eight servings.

WHAT YOU NEED:

2 eggs

2 16-ounce cans of chicken stock (or 4 cups of fresh chicken soup)

3/4 cup of uncooked rice

(continued)

3 cooking pots
spoon

WHAT YOU DO:

1. Boil the eggs in a pot of water on the stove until they are hard-boiled (about 15 minutes).
2. Remove the eggs from the pot with a spoon, cool them under cold, running water from the faucet, and then peel them. Be sure to turn off the burner when the eggs are done.
3. Cook the rice according to the directions on the package.
4. While the rice is cooking, put the stock or soup in a pan and heat it up on the stove.
5. When the rice is done, add some of the rice to the soup, depending on how thick you want the soup to be.
6. Slice or crumble the hard-boiled eggs into the soup.

It's ready!

Moroccan Green Soup

Barbara's friend, Simha Shemesh, comes from Morocco. She makes a delicious green soup for Passover, full of leeks, spinach, and other green vegetables.

Why green soup for Passover?

Green is the color of spring, so a green soup is perfect for Passover. You can make a very easy green soup in just a few minutes. This recipe makes six to eight servings.

WHAT YOU NEED:

2 16-ounce cans of chicken stock (or 4 cups of fresh chicken soup)
one bunch of scallions
1 10-ounce bag fresh spinach, chopped
salt and pepper to taste
some tasty herbs that you might like, such as 2 teaspoons of
    chopped fresh dill or cilantro
(If you wish, you can also add a cup of bite-sized pieces of other delicious Passover green vegetables, such as asparagus or broccoli.)
one-quart pot
large soup spoon
small knife for chopping
can opener

WHAT YOU DO:

1. Put the stock or soup in the pot and put it on the stove over medium heat. Bring the soup to a boil.
2. While the soup is heating up, chop the scallions into small pieces.
3. When the soup begins to boil, add the chopped scallions and spinach (and the other vegetables if you are using them) to the broth. Sprinkle in the spices and herbs, and stir.
4. Cook the soup on medium heat for 15 minutes, or until the broth turns green. Serve immediately.

STILL MORE CUSTOMS

More about Passover Foods

"We're chopping vegetables for soup."

Sephardic and Oriental Jews may also serve chicken and fish, stewed with tomatoes, vegetables, and spices.

Italian Jews (Sephardi) love pasta. But how can they eat pasta on *Pesach?* They "watch" the wheat while it's growing to make sure that extra dampness doesn't get in it. Then they form the pasta from the wheat flour, and they bake it quickly—within eighteen minutes—so it doesn't have a chance to rise.

Many non-Ashkenazic Jews *do* include lamb at the seder meal. Ethiopian Jews still make the sacrifice of the Paschal lamb and serve it at their *Pesach* feast! So do Samaritans, whose ancestors were a sect living in Palestine when the Greeks ruled the land, and who still live in Israel today. The Ethiopians and Samaritans eat their seder meal very quickly, as we are instructed in the Book of Exodus, to remember how quickly the Children of Israel had to leave *Mitzrayim.*

Dozens of cookbooks contain Passover recipes for you to make with your family. At the end of this book, you'll find Passover books with recipes just for Passover. So, try some recipes from all over the world, beginning with our favorites that we share with you on the next few pages.

CHERIE'S AND BARBARA'S FAVORITE FAMILY RECIPES

We both can remember the wonderful smells that filled our homes on Passover, as each of us helped our parents prepare the seder meals. Here are some of our favorite recipes. May they become part of your own Passover memories!

When you make these recipes, you may need to use sharp knives, a food processor, a hot oven, or a frying pan of hot oil. *Always be careful! Ask an adult to help you cook!*

Spicy Eggplant

Barbara's mom was born in Israel, when it was still called Palestine. Lots of eggplants grew there, and they ripened in the spring in time for her mom to make fried eggplant in a spicy sauce for the *Pesach* seder. This recipe makes 10 servings.

WHAT YOU NEED

2 or 3 large eggplants (Try to find dark, shiny ones!)
about 3 eggs
about 1 cup *matzah* meal
vegetable oil for frying
4 10½-ounce cans of tomato-mushroom sauce
slicing knife
bowl
plate
frying pan
paper towels
cooking pot
fork
plastic wrap

WHAT YOU DO:

1. Slice the eggplant so that you have many round slices, ¼-inch thick.
2. Crack open the eggs into a bowl. Be careful not to get the eggshells in the bowl as well! Beat the eggs with a fork.
3. Measure 1 cup of *matzah* meal and pour it on the plate.

4. Pour a little vegetable oil into the frying pan and put it on the stove on medium high.

5. While the oil is heating up, dip each piece of eggplant in the beaten egg. Dip both sides.

6. Then dip each piece in *matzah* meal until it's covered on both sides.

7. Fry the eggplant in hot oil, flipping the pieces once. Fry until each piece is soft on the inside and golden brown on the outsides. From time to time, as the oil gets absorbed into the eggplant, add another tablespoon of oil to the pan.

8. Using a fork, remove each piece and place it on a paper towel so that the towel will absorb some of the oil.

10. When all of the pieces are fried, put the eggplant in a pot and cover with the tomato-mushroom sauce.

11. Cook it on the stove until it begins to boil.

12. Turn the flame to OFF.

13. When it has cooled slightly, transfer the eggplant and sauce to a bowl and cover it with plastic wrap.

14. Place in the refrigerator to chill. Serve cold.

Sweet Israel Chicken

Cherie and her mom, Dotty, created this recipe from ingredients that can be found in Israel. It is sweet and delicious and will serve six to eight people.

WHAT YOU NEED:

25 dried apricots, cut into quarters (or you can use half apricots and half prunes)

1/2 cup chopped walnuts or almonds (buy the nuts already shelled and chopped)

1/2 cup golden or black raisins (or combine with pomegranate seeds)

3 cloves garlic, minced or pressed

1 large onion, sliced thin

4 ounces of orange or apricot preserves or marmalade

1/4 cup olive oil

1/2 cup heavy grape juice, or sweet Concord grape or blackberry Kosher wine

(continued)

1½ tablespoons vinegar

1/3 cup honey

3 pounds of chicken, cut up (white meat or dark; skin on or off)

glass baking pan, at least 10" x 17"

chopping knife

chopping board

large mixing bowl

spoon

garlic press (optional)

measuring spoons and cups

paper towels

WHAT YOU DO:

1. Preheat the oven to 350 degrees.
2. While the oven is heating, chop the apricots into quarters and place them in a large mixing bowl.
3. Measure the chopped nuts and the raisins and add them to the bowl.
4. Mash the 3 cloves of garlic in a garlic press or mince them with a knife. (Mincing means chopping into very tiny pieces.) Add the garlic to the bowl.
5. Add the sliced onion to the bowl.
6. Measure out the preserves or marmalade, olive oil, grape juice or wine, vinegar, and honey and add them to the mixing bowl.
7. Stir the ingredients together until they are well mixed.
8. Rinse the chicken pieces, pat them dry with paper towels, and lay them in the pan.
9. Pour the mixture evenly over the chicken.
10. Bake the chicken in the oven for about 1 ½ hours, or until golden brown. Check while baking to make sure that the chicken is still covered with sauce. With an adult's help, spoon the sauce over the chicken or add water, if necessary, to keep it moist. Be careful when you open the oven door because steam and heat can burn!

Passover Almond Cake

This recipe comes all the way from South Africa. From the 1930s to the early 1960s, Barbara's friend, Heinz Speier, and his brother, Kurt, owned the only kosher bakery in the city of Johannesburg. This is one of their favorite Passover cakes. It takes a lot of work, but the taste is worth it. Please have an adult help you.

WHAT YOU NEED:

6 eggs at room temperature
2 cups sugar
5 ½ ounces shelled almonds (buy ground almonds if you can)
1/2 cup potato starch (you can buy this in the supermarket)
1/3 cup sugar
1 unpeeled lemon, washed
2 tablespoons unsweetened applesauce
butter or vegetable oil for greasing the pans
measuring cups
measuring spoons
2 mixing bowls
electric mixer
food processor (to grind the almonds if you can't buy them already
    ground)
hand grater
flour sifter
long-handled spoon
paper towels
9-inch spring form pan (this is a special baking pan that has remov-
    able sides)
cookie sheet

WHAT YOU DO:

1. Preheat the oven to 350 degrees.
2. Break the eggs, putting the yolks in one bowl and the whites in another bowl. (You may need an adult to show you how to do this the first time. It is important to keep any yolk from mixing with the white.) Be careful not to drop the shells in either bowl.
3. Add 2 cups of sugar to the egg yolks. With an electric mixer, beat the egg yolks with the sugar until the mixture doubles in volume. (It takes about 15 minutes on the fast setting.)
4. In the food processor, grind the almonds until they're fine.

(continued)

"This cake needs lots of nuts."

Barbara Rush

5. Rub the unpeeled lemon against the hand grater until you have grated off the entire rind. Do not grate into the soft white part—it is quite bitter-tasting.

6. Sift the potato starch into a large bowl. Add the lemon rind and ground almonds, and stir until blended.

7. *Fold* (place gently) the egg yolk mixture into the potato starch mixture. Do not beat or mix.

8. Add the apple sauce and mix.

9. With the electric mixer, beat the 6 egg whites with 1/3 cup sugar until they form stiff peaks.

10. Put 3 tablespoons of this egg mixture into the batter and mix.

11. Add the remaining egg whites to the batter and mix until you don't see any whites.

12. Using a paper towel, spread a small amount of butter or oil on the bottom and sides of the spring fom pan.

13. Pour the batter into the pan, and place the pan on a cookie sheet. (In case the batter drips while baking, it will fall onto the cookie sheet.)

14. Bake at 350 degrees for 30 minutes. Put a toothpick into the center of the cake, and pull it out again. If the toothpick is clean, the cake is done. If not, bake for 5 more minutes.

15. Let the cake cool for at least 20 minutes before removing from the pan.

Kurt Speier says, "Put a toothpick into the center of the cake and pull it out again. If the toothpick is clean, the cake is done."

Forgotten Cookie Clouds

These cookies, made by Cherie and her mom, Dotty, are very special for Passover. They look like the clouds that the Israelites followed to find their way through the desert!

WHAT YOU NEED:

whites of two extra large eggs

2/3 cup of sugar

1/8 teaspoon salt

1 teaspoon vanilla

1 cup chopped walnuts (buy them already shelled and chopped)

3/4 cup semi-sweet chocolate bits (optional)

electric mixer
mixing bowl
cookie sheet
oil for greasing the cookie
    sheet
large spoon
paper towel

WHAT YOU DO:

1. Preheat the oven to 350 degrees.
2. Ask an adult to help you separate the egg yolks from the whites. The whites should be placed in the mixing bowl. The yolks are not needed in this recipe, but can be saved for another recipe.
3. Beat the egg whites in with a mixer until they form soft peaks.
4. This step and the next two may take two people, one to hold the mixer while the other adds the ingredients. While continuing to mix, slowly add the sugar and salt.
5. Keep mixing and add the vanilla.
6. Slowly add the walnuts and chocolate bits. Beat for 15 minutes on HIGH setting.
7. When the 15 minutes are up, stop beating the mixture. Remember to unplug the mixer.
8. With a folded paper towel, rub oil onto the cookie sheet.
9. Using a large spoon, drop a spoonful of dough at a time onto the cookie sheet, keeping the cookies two inches apart from each other.
10. Put the sheet of cookies into the oven, close the door, and *turn off the oven.*
11. Forget the cookies for a few hours! (At least three hours. Or, better yet, overnight. They are done when they are hard.)

That's why they're called "Forgotten Cookies." You just put them in the oven and forget them! But even though they're called "Forgotten Cookies," you have to remember to take them out.

That makes them a symbol that God did not forget the Jewish people. The cloud showed them the way out of the desert!

FUN

A Garbage Garden

Jewish tradition tells us that we are *Shomrei Adamah,* keepers of the earth. If we do not take care of the earth, then how will anyone or any living thing enjoy the earth after us? That's why the Torah tells us to take care of the earth, the animals, the plants, and all living things.

One way of caring for the earth is to reuse products that come from the earth. When you're cooking your *Pesach* stews and soups, what do you usually do with the tops of the vegetables? This year, instead of throwing them away, try using those "veggie" tops to grow a pretty forest garden. Here are some ideas:

Celery Trees

1. Put a small amount of water into a glass. Do the same for several glasses.
2. Place a celery stalk with leaves into each glass.
3. Add a few drops of food coloring. Use a different color for each glass.
4. After several hours the colors should reach the leaves.

A Carrot Top Plant
(Beets and parsnips may be used too.)

1. Cut off the top of the carrot, about 1 inch from the top.
2. Put the carrot top into a glass, and put 3 or 4 toothpicks into the carrot to keep the top part out of the glass.
3. Fill the glass with water until it reaches the bottom half of the carrot.
4. Change the water every few days.
5. After a few weeks, leaves will start to grow and you will have a nice plant.

Judy Lande Haran

SEDER TALK

Passover Memories

There is so much delicious food to eat during Passover! While you are enjoying your seder meal with your family and friends, take some time for Passover conversation. Here are four questions you can ask each other:

1. Who are the youngest and oldest Passover guests this year?
2. Who is new to your seder this year? What were they doing last Passover? Where did they come from?
3. What are some of your favorite Passover foods?
4. What are some Passover foods and customs that your guests may remember from long ago or far away?

Judy Lande Haran

"I hid the afikoman. Can you find it?"
Rebecca Reiman, age 11

INTRODUCTION

Whew! What a meal! Now that it's over, it's time for dessert—for the afikoman *(**ab-fee-koh-MAN**). This is the moment you've been waiting for! It's time to search! But where is it? Wait—before you start hunting through the house— did you know that the* afikoman *is more than another piece of* matzah? *After eating it, for instance, you're not supposed to eat or drink anything else for the rest of the night. Why? Keep reading . . . you'll discover how the* afikoman *can serve as a good luck piece all year long.*

STORY

Suppose the *afikoman* is nowhere to be found. It's disappeared! Read what happened in this story about Elijah the Prophet who comes, as God's messenger, to visit every Jewish home on the night of the seder. To understand the humor of this story, remember that the *afikoman* must be found before the seder can continue.

A special note: In the hundreds of folktales about Elijah the Prophet that Jews around the world tell, Elijah always knows what he is doing. He always knows where he is going. In this fictional story, Elijah is absent-minded and forgetful. But this is not the usual character of Elijah the Prophet.

Elijah's Passover Return

by Cherie Karo Schwartz and Barbara Rush

It was the eve of Passover. Elijah the Prophet had just completed his visit to every Jewish house celebrating a seder all over the world. What a job! Elijah was exhausted! Now that he had reached California, he had

finally completed his yearly task. He was ready to sink into his favorite overstuffed chair and take a well-deserved rest.

As he sat back, his mind wandered over the memories of each visit. How he loved the moment at each seder when the door was opened for him! How he loved the ways people welcomed him—the songs, the special goblet of wine set on the seder table, the special chair set aside just for him!

"Ah, it is all so very beautiful," he thought. "I never get tired of it. Every year it is a completely old and a completely new experience."

Elijah had almost drifted off to sleep when his hand brushed against something in his pocket. "What do we have here?" he said. Carefully, he reached into the pocket of his long black robe and pulled out . . . a piece of *matzah!* "Matzah? Matzah? What am I doing with a piece of *matzah?* And how did it get into my pocket?"

Elijah, who we know is very, very wise, thought and thought and thought some more. "It looks like half a piece of *matzah* . . . yes, a piece of *matzah* broken in half. But why?" From that moment, it didn't take very long for Elijah to understand what had happened. "Oy! Oy! I know what this is! It's an *afikoman!* Some little child must have hidden it behind the pillow of a chair or sofa I sat in." (After all, Elijah, who never makes mistakes, stops to rest now and then on his long journey, and it's possible that a child somewhere in the world might have accidentally placed it in his pocket, isn't it?) "This is terrible!" he cried.

Now, why would it be so terrible for Elijah to have an *afikoman?* Well, we'll tell you. We are supposed to hide the *afikoman* during the seder, then find it before we can end the seder, right? And if Elijah has the *afikoman* from somebody's seder, then that family can't finish their seder, right? "Oh, no! This is worse than terrible," Elijah said. "I've been all over the world tonight. How will I ever find out whose *afikoman* this is so I can return it in time?"

After several minutes, Elijah said, "Well, there's only one thing to do: take the *afikoman*, and start all over again, visiting one house at a time." And that is just what he did!

Off into the night went Elijah. "Probably the Jews in China, Japan, and Nepal have already finished their seders by now," he said.

Judy Lande Haran

"It's already the next day there. Still, just in case there's one family waiting . . ." And so, Elijah started off to the west. But when he got to the Far East, it was midday. The sun was shining, and there was no sign of anyone waiting to finish a seder. So on went Elijah to Israel where there were so many homes to visit. Off he went to a *kibbutz,* where hundreds of families had come together to celebrate. (Can you imagine making thousands and thousands of *matzah* balls for one seder?) But there, too, the tables had been cleared. On went Elijah through Eastern Europe, where many Jews had a seder in freedom for the very first time. Houses were dark. There was no sign of a seder still in progress! So on he flew—through Germany, France, Spain, through England and Ireland. But the seders there were over, too. By this time Elijah was becoming weary. "There's no time to rest," he thought. "I can't leave a family without their *afikoman.*" And so, taking a deep breath, Elijah crossed the ocean, then went up and down the coast, from the northern tip of Canada to the bottom of Argentina. He found many families whose songs were finished, and whose guests had already left; dishes were being cleaned, and no one seemed to be looking for a missing piece of *matzah.*

Now, an ordinary person might have become discouraged, but not Elijah. After all, he was used to doing extraordinary things. So, taking a deep breath, Elijah went on through Chicago and St. Louis, through the farmlands of the Midwest. Everywhere Elijah went, he saw again the beauty of each seder. What he didn't see was a family in need of their *afikoman!* Time was running out!

As he came to the mountains of Colorado, Elijah was so weary that even he was almost ready to give up. But then, as he passed over the city of Denver, he suddenly heard a beautiful young voice singing Passover songs. So he followed the sound of singing and came to a small house overflowing with tables, chairs, family, and friends. There was singing and laughter and talking. The seder tables were all different sizes and shapes, with all different colors of tablecloths, surrounded by many kinds of chairs with people of many ages. It all looked . . . absolutely lovely! "Yes, I think that I remember this house. There was something very special here." Then he saw in the corner, away from the rest of the jumble of chairs and tables, a single chair by itself. It was made of wood and had a worn-looking red velvet cushion. No one was sitting in it. "Ah, yes," sighed Elijah, as he sat down in the chair himself.

But Elijah could not rest. Inside that house the room buzzed in confusion. People stood at the very chair where Elijah was sitting (but, of course, they could not see him). Elijah listened. In the midst of the noise, one small girl's voice could be heard. "But that *is* where I hid the *afikoman*," she cried. "Right there in the tear in the seat cushion. I thought it was a perfect place because that is Elijah's chair!"

"That's right," thought Elijah, "some families set a special chair at the seder table in my honor! . . . Aha! That may be how I got the *afikoman* in my pocket!" (And, luckily, Elijah's *afikoman* didn't crumble, even if he sat on it!)

"Now think again, Sari," said the girl's mother. "It isn't here, and you were the last child to have it."

"Yeah, and you know we can't finish the seder until we find the *afikoman*," said her big brother, Benjy. "Come on, it's getting late."

"This night is really different from all other nights."
Rebecca Reiman, age 11

"Maybe Sari doesn't really remember," her father said. "Let's take one last look around the living room." Off he went with the seder guests to search the house while five-year-old Sari started to cry.

That was just the moment Elijah had been waiting for. Quicker than you can say *"charoset,"* Elijah slipped the *afikoman* out of his pocket and into the tear in the red velvet material. Sari's mother was standing next to her, trying to comfort her. Suddenly, she gasped and pointed at the chair. When Sari lifted her head, she could hardly believe her eyes! *"Look! Look!"* she cried. Everyone in the house came running. There was the *afikoman!*

"Sari, did you just put that back? What a trick!" cried Benjy.

"No," said her mother, "she was nowhere near it. I'm the one who saw it first, but how did it get back here?"

Everyone was talking at once. Then Sari looked at the worn-down creases in the cushion. Someone had sat in that chair! "I know what happened. I put the *afikoman* in Elijah's chair, and it magically disappeared. Now Elijah has brought it back. Elijah really was here, *really!* And he wanted us to know he came to our house."

"Well, I will say something. It's a wonder that we can finish our seder! Everybody back to your seats, and let's finish up. It's really late!" said her father.

And so, after all the children had received coins for redeeming the *afikoman,* and after songs and greetings of "*L'shanah Ha'ba'ah B'Yerushalayim*—Next year in Jerusalem" had been exchanged, another seder came to an end. On her way back to her chair, Sari was humming the song "*Eliyahu ha Navi,*" for that was her favorite. She was so sleepy that she rested her head on her mother's shoulder and drifted off to sleep.

As for Elijah, he took a sip of wine from the special cup set aside for him and fell fast asleep, too. He was exhausted from his long journey, and deserved a rest. Don't you think so?

Note to the storyteller: You may want to have Elijah return the *afikoman* to the city where you live.

CRAFT
An Afikoman Bag

How do you hide the *afikoman?* Do you wrap it in a napkin first? Here are directions for making a special *afikoman* bag that you can use year after year at your seders.

WHAT YOU NEED:

a piece of soft fabric (like cotton), 14"x 8½"
needle and thread (in a color to match the fabric)
sewing pins
scissors
piece of Velcro, a button, or snap

WHAT YOU DO:

1. Lay the fabric out on a table, right side up.
2. Fold the long side up so that it is double material for 10 inches, leaving a 4-inch deep single layer of fabric at the top.

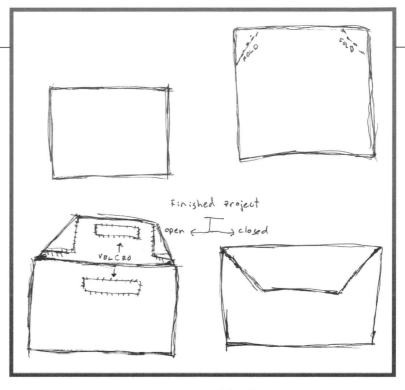

Larry Schwartz

3. Turn the material inside out, and using a whipstitch, sew the "pocket" (double material part) together on three sides, leaving the 4-inch left-over material side open for the top of the envelope.

4. Sew a hem on the top of this open side by folding the edge under 1/4 inch and then folding it under another 1/4 inch. Pin it in place as you fold so that the folds do not come undone. Then whipstitch the fold to the fabric. Ask an adult to show you how to do the whipstitch.

5. On the 4-inch top of the envelope, fold (tuck) the outside corners down on the diagonal to make the top of the envelope and sew them down flat with several whipstitches each.

6. Sew a snap or pieces of Velcro in the middle of the top flap and the envelope so that the bag will close. Or, cut a buttonhole in the middle of the top flap and whipstitch around the cut edges of the hole. Then close the top flap over the envelope and stick a pin through the buttonhole into the envelope fabric below. This will mark the place where you should sew the button.

CUSTOMS

Four Afikoman Questions

After the meal, we seek out the hidden *afikoman;* we see that what is lost can yet be found, completed, made whole.

? How can you find and ransom the *afikoman?*

Each family has different traditions. If the children hide the *afikoman,* the adults must search for it. If the adults can't find the *afikoman,* they have to give the children a gift to redeem (buy back) the *afikoman.*

If an adult hides the *afikoman,* the children must search for it. When the children find the *afikoman,* they can refuse to give it back unless they get a gift.

If you hide fake *afikoman* pieces around the house or give clues in rhyme, you can enjoy searching for the real *afikoman*. This game shows that it is not always easy to find the right solution or to put broken things together.

Some families redeem the *afikoman* with money or a gift. Sometimes this is given only to the child who finds the *afikoman* but it may be given to all the children at the seder.

? What happens to the *afikoman* after it is found?

We place the two halves of the *matzah* together and see the whole once more. The leader then distributes pieces of the *afikoman,* and everyone must eat a piece. This is the dessert that ends the meal, after which nothing more may be eaten that night. Now the seder may continue.

? How can the *afikoman* be good luck for the future?

The *afikoman* is a reminder of our people's *past* in Egypt. But many people believe that the *afikoman* can also bring good luck for the future.

Jews in some parts of the world believe that after part of the *afikoman* is eaten, the remainder should be hidden in the pages of the *Haggadah,* or in containers of flour, rice, and salt, or in a drawer, or in a coat pocket. The *afikoman* is hidden for the whole year to bring blessings and abundance.

Other Jews believe that the *afikoman* should be displayed to bring good luck. In many Sephardic communities, people used to wear a piece of *afikoman* around their necks like a good luck charm. During the Middle Ages in Europe, the *afikoman* was hung in the house for everyone to see.

? How can you help make broken things whole again?

How will you answer this question?

SEDER TALK
Making Things Whole

There are probably some projects in your house that you've been wanting to complete, but you just haven't gotten around to them yet. Take a lesson from the *afikoman,* and plan to finish at least one of them in the "in between" days of Passover. In fact, you can make this a family project.

After the second day of Passover, post a special "sign-up sheet" in your house. Have each family member write down at least one project that needs completion. Does your room need cleaning? Do papers need sorting? Do shelves need to be straightened? Does something need repair or painting? As the week goes by, cross off the tasks as you complete them, and feel great about completing them!

During the "in between" days of Passover, invite some neighbors to a meeting at your house. Decide on some neighborhood projects that are in need of completion. Does the park need work? Do the streets need to be cleaned of trash or graffiti? Or is there a community building in need of repair? Decide on a specific project, and follow it through to completion.

Making things whole is very important in Judaism. This is called *tikkun olam,* which means repairing the world.

POEM

The Great Afikoman Search

Our seder meal's all finished.
It's time for our dessert,
to join our friends and cousins
in the *afikoman* search.

We need that *afikoman*
to make a broken *matzah* whole,
so our seder can continue with
more songs and fun for all.

But the *afikoman*'s hidden.
Wherever can it be?
Oh, I wish the *afikoman*
would show itself to me!

Then I would be the hero
and get a prize or two
for finding the half *matzah*.
Our searching would be through!
(continued on p. 151)

Searching for the afikoman—is it under the rug?

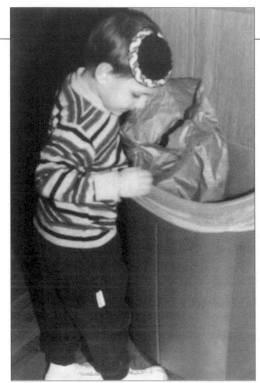

...in the garbage?

...in the drawer?

...under the plant?

"I found it!"

But I've looked throughout the kitchen,
over windows, behind beds;
I've checked the hallway closet,
under chairs and overhead.

Where can that *afikoman* be?
On the porch? Indoors? Outside?
If *you* were the *afikoman,*
where would *you* want to hide?

BIRKAT HAMAZON: SAYING GRACE AFTER THE MEAL

After eating our "dessert" of *afikoman*—the last bit of food that we eat at the seder—we thank God for the food and other good things that God has given us. This prayer of special thanks is called the "Blessing of the Food." In Hebrew, it's known as *Birkat Hamazon.*

When we sing or recite *Birkat Hamazon,* we are thanking God for four things:

- for giving food to all people;
- for giving us the Land of Israel;
- for giving us Jerusalem, God's holy city;
- for giving good things to every individual person.

Part of the blessing says: "Blessed be God who feeds the whole world with grace, love, and compassion. Through God's goodness we have never known the lack of food. . . . Blessed be God, who feeds us all."

You can find the words of *Birkat Hamazon* in your *Haggadah.*

Father recites the Birkat . . .
Geismar Haggadah, Germany, 1928

Who's dozing off?

Judy Lande Haran

Singing Praises and Concluding the Seder

Take a deep breath—and then open your *Haggadah* again. Now that you've finished the festive meal, you can continue the seder with prayers to God of praise and thanksgiving.

If you remember, we began the seder by recalling the slavery of the Jews in Egypt, but we end by looking forward to a future of freedom, understanding, and peace. With help from the Prophet Elijah, bringer of hope to those in need, we move toward Jerusalem and the Land of Israel in our hearts and in our lives.

We began this book with the ancient Exodus from Egypt. Now we tell the story of some modern exoduses as Jews from around the world continue to seek freedom—and peace—in Israel.

Elijah the Prophet.
Lucy Schwartz, age 15

INTRODUCTION

Every year at Passover you may open the door for Elijah and welcome him to your seder. But do you know who Elijah is and why we wait for him?

Elijah was a prophet who lived in Israel almost three thousand years ago. Some legends say that he could predict the future and heal the sick. He helped people, especially children, in trouble, and he told about the goodness of God. If you read about Elijah in the Bible (I Kings and II Kings), you will discover that Elijah did not die. Instead, he rose to heaven in a fiery chariot.

So, people believe that Elijah can return to earth as God's messenger from time to time to help people in need, especially those who keep the mitzvot *(commandments) and who want to celebrate the holidays. Many stories are told about Elijah and his wonderful deeds. In these stories Elijah does many things. For example, he makes peace between parents and children. He brings Shabbat candles to people who can't afford to buy them. And he sends money (gold coins) so people can celebrate good occasions and the holidays, especially Passover seders, with joy.*

Jews all over the world love Elijah so much that they have told more than six hundred different stories about him. Do you know that more folktales are told about Elijah than about any other Jewish hero? There are even more stories about Elijah than about Moses or King Solomon!

In the stories Elijah usually wears a disguise so that no one knows when or how he may appear. Very often he comes as an old man, wearing a long black coat and leaning on a walking stick. Hundreds of years ago the rabbis taught that Elijah will come to announce the time of the Messiah. Legend says that the Gate of Mercy in Jerusalem, which is now closed, will open so that Elijah may enter the city. Then there will be a time of peace—no more wars and no more quarrels.

An artist's vision: Elijah the Prophet and the Messiah going into Jerusalem.
Mantua Haggadah, Italy, c. 1560

Do you see what this has to do with Passover? It's at Passover that we gather together with family and friends, the holiday when we think of freedom and of making a better world. At our seder we open the door and welcome Elijah, hoping that this year he will bring us—and all Israel—peace.

STORY

Almost every family has a special cup for Elijah, which they set out for him every year at their seders. The cup in this story is truly very special.

The Treasured Cup of Elijah

A folktale from the Ukraine, retold by Barbara Rush

In the Ukraine (**You-CRANE**), in the city of Sakbir, there once lived a Jew named Dovid, his wife, Sarah, and their three children.

Now, Dovid was a woodcutter. Every morning, even in the heaviest rain and bitterest cold, he would cut down trees, chop the branches into small logs, and sell them to the Jews of the city. And so his family had enough money to celebrate the holidays.

But one winter was unusually cold. Snow fell for weeks and weeks, covering the streets, clogging the roads, and piling itself up against the doorways of houses. No one could go out until the snow stopped. Dovid sat at home, day after day, watching the snow fall, reading from Psalms, and praying for a miracle. But reading Psalms did not bring food to the mouths of his family. Soon they finished the last bits of lentils, beans, and potatoes they had stored away for winter.

After *Purim,* the snow stopped, and the woodcutter returned to work. But Dovid had not worked for weeks. Now he earned only enough money to keep his wife and children from starving.

Then, to make life even more difficult, a new problem arose. The holiday of *Pesach* was approaching, and Dovid did not have enough money to make even one seder. Where would he get *matzos,* wine, clothes for the family? *Pesach* without a seder was absolutely unthinkable! And so, as the days passed and the holiday grew nearer, Dovid watched his neighbors prepare all sorts of good recipes for the seder, while he continued to read from Psalms and to pray.

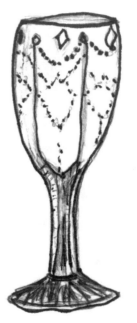

Ben Solovey, age 11

Stephanie Hays, age 11

One week before *Pesach,* Dovid's wife, Sarah, came to him. "My dear husband," she said, "reading Psalms will not help put *matzos* on our seder table. Take the silver Cup of Elijah that once belonged to your parents, and sell it. With the money we can buy all that we need for the holiday."

But Dovid refused. He remembered how the Cup of Elijah had stood on the seder table every year of his life. How he himself had watched wide-eyed each seder night to see if the Prophet Elijah would drink some of the wine set aside for him. How his mother had polished the cherished cup, year after year.

"No!" he cried. "I will not sell Elijah's Cup. God will send us a miracle, and we will celebrate *Pesach* like all other Jews."

One day, two days, passed. Finally, the woodcutter went to the rabbi. Tearfully, he told the rabbi how his wife wanted him to sell the Cup of Elijah to buy food for the holiday. But how could he sell the sacred object that had been a treasure in his family?

The rabbi listened, stroked his beard, and said, "Reb Dovid, don't worry. God's help will come." Then he went to the *tzedakah* (charity) box, took out a few silver coins, and handed them to the woodcutter. "I'm sure the day will come," he said, "when you will be able to return this."

Dovid humbly thanked the rabbi. Clutching the silver coins in his hand, he turned to go.

"There is one more thing," the rabbi said. "Don't tell anyone—anyone at all—where the money came from."

Dovid did as the rabbi asked. His family was overjoyed at the sight of the coins. The night of the seder came, and the table was prepared according to Jewish law: *matzos,* wine, *charoses,* and all the other sym-

Ben Solovey, age 11

bols of our people's slavery and freedom. As they had done for so many
years, the family read the story from
the *Haggadah*. Then, when it came
time for the youngest son to open
the door, into the room came an old
man whose long beard grew down to his knees. The man quickly
picked up the Cup of Elijah, and tasted the wine.

"Welcome, welcome to our seder," cried Dovid. "Won't you stay
and participate with us?"

"Oh, no," said the old man, "I would like very much to stay, but I
have so many other families to visit." And so, as quickly as the man
had come, he went on his way.

The next day, Dovid again went to visit the rabbi. Dovid told him
of the elderly guest who had come to his seder. Instead of showing any
surprise, the rabbi simply smiled and answered, "Oh, yes. The same old
man came to visit our seder, too!" He didn't think there was anything
unusual in a poor man seeking a little warm food or drink on a holiday.

All during the holiday, Dovid was full of happiness. Still, he knew
that he had to repay the money he had borrowed from the rabbi. But
how?

After *Pesach,* Dovid returned to the forest to work. When he drew
back the branches to make a path, he stumbled over a large, oddly-
shaped rock that was covered with snow. With his heavy mitten, Dovid
cleared away the snow, and blinked his eyes in
disbelief. It was not a rock at all, but a large sack
filled with gold! Dovid could not imagine where
it had come from. Nevertheless, he was overjoyed at his newly found riches.

The loan from the *tzedakah* box was quickly
repaid. Dovid often filled the box to overflowing
to help the rabbi help others who were in need.
For all the days of his life, Dovid remembered
that seder evening. He was certain that the old
guest at his seder was none other than Elijah the
Prophet, who had blessed Dovid and his family
because he, Dovid the woodcutter, had refused
to sell the Cup of Elijah the Prophet.

Why is the Cup of Elijah so important to Dovid?
What makes the cup special?

Why do you think the rabbi lent the money
to Dovid? Why didn't he give Dovid the money
as a gift? Why didn't the rabbi want Dovid to
tell anyone where the money came from?

At the end of the story, after Dovid became
rich, why did he give money to the rabbi to
give to other Jews? Why didn't Dovid himself
give money to other Jews?

Coby Gould, age 12

CUSTOMS

Welcoming Elijah

At most seders, when the door is opened for Elijah, a cup filled with wine is waiting for him on the seder table. At some seders, there is even a special place—plate, fork, spoon, and knife—set at the table or a special chair set aside for him. These traditions inspire us with hope that Elijah will come one day to all our tables, everywhere, announcing peace.

There are many ways that Jews around the world welcome Elijah to the seder:

After the Festive Meal, we open the door for Elijah and invite him to the seder. In some communities, when the door is opened, everyone stands up together. In other communities, the door is left open throughout the seder. This is not only for Elijah, but also for any person who is hungry to come and eat.

The Cup of Elijah

Ashkenazic Jews and many Sephardic and Oriental Jews set a cup for Elijah at the seder table. They fill the cup with wine for him to drink. Hassidic Jews—followers of the teachings of the Baal Shem Tov, a great Jewish leader in Poland in the eighteenth century—have a different custom. They pass an *empty* cup around the seder table, and everyone pours into it a little bit of wine from his or her own cup. This shows that we can each contribute something to help make the world better.

In Holland wine is poured into the Cup of Elijah and then a piece of the *afikoman* is placed for him on top of the cup. In that way Elijah can also finish the seder.

Tradition says that we can tell that Elijah has come to the seder because he drinks a bit of wine from his cup! Have you ever watched the Cup of Elijah after opening the door to see if any wine has disappeared?

This Elijah's Cup, from the former Czechoslovakia, was taken by the Nazis during World War II and found by its owners after the war.

A Chair for Elijah

Some families set aside a special chair for Elijah to sit in when he arrives.

SONG

Eliyahu ha Navi (Elijah's Song)

At many seders, the song *"Eliyahu ha Navi"* (**Eh-lee-AH-hoo hah na-VEE**), is sung in Hebrew or English as the door is opened.

Elijah the Prophet
Elijah the Tishbite from Gilead.
He will soon be here
with the Messiah,
the son of David.

Elijah the Prophet, Elijah the Tishbite, Elijah of Gilead:
may he soon come and bring the Messiah

אֵלִיָּהוּ הַנָּבִיא, אֵלִיָּהוּ הַתִּשְׁבִּי,
אֵלִיָּהוּ, אֵלִיָּהוּ, אֵלִיָּהוּ הַגִּלְעָדִי,
בִּמְהֵרָה בְּיָמֵינוּ יָבֹא אֵלֵינוּ
עִם מָשִׁיחַ בֶּן דָּוִד.

Zak dressed up to look like Elijah.

SEDER TALK
Opening the Door

What are we doing when we open the door for Elijah? What are some things that we can open the door to?

We can open the door to welcome spring into our lives after the long winter; we can open our arms to welcome the stranger; we can open our minds to new ideas; and, we can open our hearts to family, friends, and new people.

FUN
Elijah Buddies

Write the name of each of your seder guests on small pieces of paper. Then put all the names into a box. Have each person draw one name out of the box. This will be the name of his or her secret pal. During the next month, each person will do one *secret* act of kindness or make a special surprise to help that person. What fun it will be to be Elijahs for each other!

Has anyone ever helped you at just the right time? When you were sad? Sick? In trouble? Maybe someone was being a secret "Elijah" for you. Have you thought about how you can be Elijah-like for other people?

You can do small deeds of kindness (*gemilut chasadim*—**gehm-ee-LUTE chass-ah-DEEM**) *without any one else knowing*. Then you would really be like the Prophet Elijah.

Here are some more ideas. Try to think of others that would be just right.

• IN YOUR FAMILY: Do the chore that someone didn't have time to do, leave a cheery note for someone having a hard time, make someone's bed (even your brother's or sister's!), or leave a surprise such as a flower or a drawing in a special place.

• IN YOUR NEIGHBORHOOD: Pick up the newspapers of vacationing neighbors so strangers won't know that they are out of town, pick

Steven opens the door and says, "Welcome, Elijah!"

up trash in the street to make it cleaner, leave flowers or a small gift for someone who is ill or unhappy.

- IN YOUR COMMUNITY: Join in a project to help make repairs in a house of someone in need, help paint over graffiti or participate in a community mural painting project, leave bags of food or supplies at a shelter (without telling anyone).

What other projects can you think of and do?

CRAFTS

Elijah's Cup

You can create a beautiful cup for Elijah's wine for your own seder table.

WHAT YOU NEED:

plastic wine glass
magic markers or paints

WHAT YOU DO:

Draw or paint different symbols or letters on the cup. Here are some ideas, but you can create your own design:

1. Hebrew or English letters for Elijah.
2. Colors and symbols of freedom.
3. A cluster of grapes for wine.
4. An open door for Elijah.

A Clay Elijah's Cup

WHAT YOU NEED:

a plastic or paper cup (small or medium-sized, depending on how large you want your cup to be)

self-hardening clay (Clay usually comes in 5-pound packages. You won't need to use all of it to make the cup, so share some with friends or have fun making another project such as the Clay Figures craft on page 167.)

Judy Lande Haran

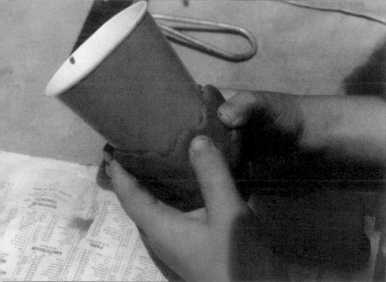

water-based paint (tempera or acrylic). Use silver or gold or choose a bright color.

1/4 inch paintbrush (the kind that comes in a watercolor kit)

WHAT YOU DO:

1. Spread some old newspapers on a large, flat surface. Place the plastic or paper cup upside down on the paper.
2. Make little balls of clay as big as large grapes, and then flatten them into "pancakes."
3. Press the clay "pancakes" all around the sides of the cup until the plastic or paper is completely covered. You may find it easier to hold the cup in one hand while you pat the clay in place with the other. If needed, you can use your finger to apply a bit of water to the edges of the "pancakes" to help them stick together.
4. Make a golf-ball-sized ball of clay, and flatten it into a big "pancake."
5. Cover the bottom of the cup with the big clay "pancake." Make sure that the bottom clay is attached to the clay on the sides of the cup. Use a bit of water here, too, to make the edges stick together.
6. Leave the clay to dry for about 24 hours.
7. When the clay is dry, carefully remove the plastic cup. *The clay will be hard, so the cup should come out easily.*
8. Paint the clay cup. You may use a Star of David, the name of Elijah, or any other design you choose.
9. After the paint is dry, return the plastic cup to the inside of the clay cup so that when you pour in the wine, you will pour it into the paper or plastic cup.

Welcome Blessing Placemat

You can write a special blessing to welcome Elijah's spirit into your home.

WHAT YOU NEED:

a piece of cardboard, posterboard, or heavy paper, about 12" x 18", big enough to use as a placemat under your Elijah Cup

pens or magic markers

Cherie Karo Schwartz

WHAT YOU DO:

Write a message of blessing to welcome Elijah. Here are some ideas, or create your own special blessing:

1. "Welcome to our seder, Elijah, bringer of peace."
2. "As we open the door to you, may doors of freedom be opened to all people everywhere."
3. "Elijah, you bless us with your presence."
4. "Elijah, tell us a story of freedom."

MORE SEDER TALK

Hallel

"Hallelujah! Praise the name of God!"

These are words from Psalm 113 from the Book of Psalms in the Bible. After we open the door for Elijah, we sing these words of praise to God, along with many other beautiful words of praise that were written long ago in the days when the Holy Temple stood in Jerusalem.

Together, these words of praise are called *Hallel,* which means "praise" in Hebrew. Other psalms recited as part of the *Hallel* at the seder are Psalms 115, 116, 117, 118, and 136. Can you find them in your Bible or in your *Haggadah*?

There Are Many Ways of Traveling to Eretz Yisrael.

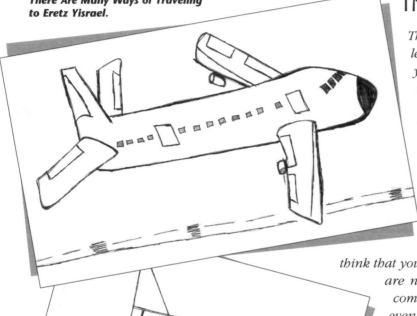

Leah Glass, age 12

INTRODUCTION

The Haggadah *tells how the Jewish people left Egypt and went to Israel thousands of years ago. Since the Exodus of long ago, many Jews from countries all over the world have made the journey to Israel, too. Since 1948, when the State of Israel was formally established, millions of Jews have come to Israel. Why did they leave their own countries? How did they get to Israel?*

We have all wandered on journeys, just as the Children of Israel wandered after leaving Egypt. Do you think that your own family has always lived where they are now? Most probably not! They may have come from a different city, state, country, or even continent! In this chapter, you'll read many people's immigration stories. And you will learn how to find out more about your own family's immigration story, too.

STORY

How lucky we are to be able to read this story! Why? Because even though many stories have been told by Jews from such places as Russia and Poland, or from Morocco, Iran, Iraq, and Yemen, we have only a small number of stories told by Jews from Ethiopia. This story, told by Moshe Taazazo from Ethiopia, is one of them.

Do you know that this is a true story?

The exodus to Jerusalem that is described in this story took place in 1862 when the British fought the Ethiopian emperor, Theodorus. The story is very special because it shows how a story—a story about a real event or a hero—can keep hope alive.

An Exodus Story: A Tale from Ethiopia

Retold by Barbara Rush

It happened about 130 years ago, when Emperor Theodorus ruled Ethiopia, that foreign armies came to the land. And so the emperor called forth his many soldiers—Christians, Moslems, and Jews—to help defeat the enemy. Now, the Jews asked to fight separately as a unit, so that they could keep the *mitzvot* (commandments) of the Torah. And they did—they ate the food allowed by law and prayed to God—and it happened that the Jews were successful in battle. Their enemies quickly fled from their path.

The emperor was pleased and called for the leader of the Jews, whose name was Aba Mahari (**A-bah mah-HAHR-ee**), a Cohen, to appear before him. "I wish to thank you," said the emperor. "Tell me, what gift can I bestow upon you?"

Aba Mahari replied, "Your Majesty, we do not want money, gold, or any wealth in Ethiopia. What we seek is permission to go to the Land of Israel, to Jerusalem."

To this request the emperor declared, "I would miss such great fighters. For haven't I seen with my own eyes how the enemy fled from your soldiers? Such victories must be due to your faith in your God. But, to show how much I thank you, I will grant your request." And so a decree was sent throughout the land: The Jews of Ethiopia may go forth to Jerusalem.

Soon the word was spread through Gondar, Dembia, and all of Ethiopia. Thousands of Jews—men and women, children and older people—gathered together for the journey. How happy they were! Quickly they gathered food and drink, sheep and goats, blankets and clothing. Soon they began their march full of joy and hope that they would be able to cross *Yam-Suf* (The Red Sea), as had the Children of Israel, thousands of years before when they set forth from Egypt.

But as the weeks passed, the rains fell and many died. Some died of sickness. Some turned back. Most of the people marched on until they reached the shores of the Red Sea. There they stood, the men, women, babies, and old folks, on the banks of the sea, led by Aba Mahari. This was just how the Children of Israel must have stood, they thought, led by Moses so many years before.

Aba Mahari, the Cohen, raised his staff, and struck the water. The

Yoni Dinur, age 13

people waited, but the waters did not part. Again, Aba Mahari raised his staff and struck the water. He tried a third time. But the waters did not move.

And so, sad and disappointed, the men, women, and children began the long walk back to their villages. They were tired, hungry, and weak. Throughout the journey Aba Mahari remained with his people, giving them comfort, and leading them in prayer. And the people thought, "God does not want us to enter the Land of Israel at this time. But we will continue to pray for freedom. Some day we—or our children or our children's children—will enter Jerusalem!"

The Exodus of Aba Mahari was over. His people did not come to Jerusalem in their lifetime. But the story of Aba Mahari and his people was told in Ethiopia in every generation. Parents told it to their children. Those children told it to their children. In this way hope was kept alive. And now that I—and my family and thousands of other Ethiopians—have crossed the Red Sea in our time and have come to the city of Jerusalem, we continue to tell the story of Aba Mahari and his brave people. Because of them, because of their story, we have arrived.

The story also shows that the Jews of Ethiopia, like Jews all over the world, longed to return to *Eretz Yisrael,* to Jerusalem. Today thousands of Jews still remain in Ethiopia. They would like to come to *Eretz Yisrael,* too, but the Ethiopian government will not let them go. Can you offer a prayer for them? Talk to your family about what else you can do to help them become free.

Ethiopian immigrants study Hebrew in Israel.

CRAFTS

Clay Figures

The Ethiopian Jews (like the ones in the story) used clay for making things, and you can, too.

Get Marblex, Fimo, Sculpie, or some other self-hardening clay. Make a statue out of the clay that looks like someone who has come from a different country. Use the leftover clay to put some special clothes or jewelry or hat on the figure to show where the person has come from. If you are having a hard time thinking of what to make, you might want to make a figure of a Near Eastern man all dressed up for the part of the seder about the Exodus—with a long robe, a walking stick, and a pack on his back (representing an Israelite wandering in the desert). Then, bake the figure or let it dry according to the directions supplied with the clay. Each year, you can add more clay figures, so you can build a collection of Jewish dolls from all over the world!

Immigration Tiles

At a store, buy a light-colored tile that is at least four inches square. At home, use oil paints to create a scene on the tile that shows a story about someone coming to a new land or someone going to Israel. Or at a crafts store you can buy special colored pencils that you can use to write on your tile.

Try to make the people look like they came from another country, and include many things about their clothes and the environment. You can use the tile for decoration at the seder table or on the wall.

Larry Schwartz

SEDER TALK

Other Exoduses to Eretz Yisrael

Many people from around the world have gone to live in Israel. Emigration means leaving a country, and immigration means coming into a country. Between 1948 and 1995, Jews from 102 different countries emigrated from (left) their homelands and immigrated (came) to Israel. Here are some of these exoduses:

Immigrants from Morocco arrive by boat, 1952.

FROM	NUMBER
the former Soviet Union	more than 800,000 (600,000 from 1990–1995)
North Africa (Morocco, Egypt, Algiers, Tunisia, Libya)	420,000 (most came in the 1950s)
Iraq	130,000
Iran	76,000
United States	71,000
Yemen	51,000 (many came in 1959)
Ethiopia	49,000 (more than 20,000 came in 1991)
Argentina	44,000
France	31,000
India	27,000
the former Yugoslavia	10,000

Sometimes, when the government of Israel brings large numbers of Jews out of other countries to live in Israel, they give the projects special names like these:

Operation Magic Carpet

Operations Ezra and Nechemiah

Operation Moses

Operation Solomon

Can you match these names with the countries that the Jews came from?

ANSWERS:

OPERATION MAGIC CARPET:
Yemen (1949–1950)

OPERATIONS EZRA AND
NECHEMIAH: Iraq (1950–1951)

OPERATION MOSES: Ethiopia
(1984–1985)

OPERATION SOLOMON:
Ethiopia (1991)

IMMIGRATION STORIES

Many people have visited Israel, and some of them have decided to live in Israel. Have you ever been to Israel? Has anyone in your family? Do you know any Israeli people? Do you have any relatives in Israel? Can you find someone with an "Israel connection"? Talk with them about what it is like to live in Israel or to move there.

Here are four interesting stories about people who have moved from other countries to Israel.

From Yemen (YEH-men)

In 1948, after the State of Israel was established, the situation for the Jews in Yemen was very dangerous. They were treated very badly by their neighbors and by the government in their country. The Israeli government decided to send airplanes to bring thousands of Jews from Yemen to Israel. This was called Operation Magic Carpet. Barbara's friend, Ziporah Sibahi Greenfield, remembers:

Operation Magic Carpet, 1949—bringing Yemenite Jews to Israel.

"My parents watched as the great airplanes swooped down amidst us. They had never seen an airplane before, and they thought, 'This is a giant bird that has been sent by God to take us to *Eretz Yisrael*.' They climbed on, with their children and a few of their possessions, and soon afterward landed in Israel, their new home."

From Egypt

Jews lived in Egypt for thousands of years, but they were not allowed to become citizens, with all of the rights of other Egyptians. In 1949, the Egyptian government made life so hard for Jews that almost all the Jews left the country. Cherie's friend, Dr. Ada Aharoni, remembers:

"I remember . . . the last seder in our family in Cairo (in 1949). . . . I asked, 'Why do we thank God for taking us out of Egypt if we are still here?' . . . Nona (grandmother) Regina smiled and said in the old Ladino (language combining Spanish and Hebrew) she loved, '*El Dio es tadroso, ma no es oulvidiso!* God is sometimes late, but never forgets!' . . . A week later, my father's permit to work in Egypt was cancelled. . . . And so, my own exodus from Egypt to Israel, through France, began, as we were not allowed to travel straight from Egypt to Israel. It was sad to leave my friends, my school, my books, the Nile, the pyramids, and our wonderful neighbors, but it was also exciting to go to Israel."

From Romania

Barbara's friend, Doron Elia, says: "When World War II started, my grandma, Sonny, decided to leave Romania and go to Palestine, the Holy Land. She dressed herself in an elegant white dress with pearls and a fancy hat, and she began to walk. But, unfortunately, it took Grandma many years to get there. She was put into a concentration camp, escaped, walked by foot across the mountains to Italy, was captured again, and finally was freed at the end of the war. Grandma finally made her way to Palestine (as Israel was known before 1948); and, before she entered, she dressed in an elegant dress, so that she could at last enter the Holy Land properly."

From Poland

In the year 1921, when he was nineteen years old, Barbara's father, Abraham Wishengrad, decided to go to Palestine to help build a land for the Jewish people. He and a small group of young men—and women, too—from his village had to go first to the city of Vienna in Austria. In Vienna, they had to wait for permission to enter Palestine. While they were there, they went to visit the grave of Theodor Herzl, who was one of the first to dream that Jews might rebuild their own homeland in Palestine one day. Herzl said, "If you wish it, it need not be a dream." Those are the words (in Hebrew) that you see on the left-hand side of the photo. These words became the slogan for young Jewish men and women, like Barbara's father, who were going to

AFTER THE STATE OF ISRAEL WAS ESTABLISHED IN 1948, THE GRAVE OF THEODOR HERZL WAS MOVED TO JERUSALEM. IF YOU GO TO JERUSALEM, YOU CAN VISIT IT IN A LARGE CEMETERY CALLED HAR HERZL.

Palestine. They worked hard to farm the land and to build cities so that we could have the State of Israel today.

PROJECTS

Gathering Family Stories

The stories of our Jewish people have been with us for thousands of years. Wherever Jews have lived around the world, our stories have traveled with us: stories of holidays, good deeds, charity, and justice. Our family stories have traveled through time and place, too. They are our families' precious treasures. As we learn and tell our family stories, we are preserving our family memories and history.

The young man with the canteen on the far right is Barbara's father.

Be a family story detective. How can you gather your family's stories? How can you preserve them and tell them? Here are some ideas:

Before Passover, interview members of your family. Use a tape recorder, or take notes.

Who is the oldest? Youngest?

What are some favorite Passover memories? Foods? Customs?

What are some other holidays and joyous celebrations they remember?

What are some special foods in your family?

Immigration stories (how people traveled from place to place) are very important parts of your family history. See if you can find out:

What are some other cultures or countries in your family history?

How did your family get to the state or country where you live?

How did they travel? What were some of their adventures along the way?

Ask people who have come from other places:

Where and when were you born?

When and why did you decide to leave?

Do you remember the journey to the new place? What was it like? Were you scared?

Did you take anything special with you?

Our First Day in America! In the 1990s Avraham Hebrew and his family, one of the few Jewish families in Pakistan, immigrated to the U.S.

After you have gathered family stories, write them down and collect them in a looseleaf binder. Create a cover design that tells something about your family. Have your Family Stories notebook at your seder so that people can share their stories. The seder guests may give you more stories, and each year you can add new family stories to the notebook. Here is a story that Cherie tells about her grandmother's own immigration from England to the United States:

"My grandmother, Rae (born Rachel) Cohen Olesh, came from London, England. She lived from 1893 to 1983, ninety full years. During World War I her boyfriend was killed in the war and her father died. This was such a shock that she lost her voice! Every time she tried to say something, she couldn't speak at all.

"She came to the United States on a huge boat with one of her sisters. In the middle of the ocean, the ship was caught in a terrible storm and the boat almost sank! She went onto the deck, opened her mouth, and tried to sing the words of the English national anthem, 'God Save the King.' Like a miracle, her voice returned and the ship was saved.

"She came through Ellis Island in New York. Then she took a train to Denver, where she met and married Isadore Olesh, and they had many children and grandchildren. Many of them are still in Denver. You should see the size of our seders!"

Can you discover similar treasures in your family's history?

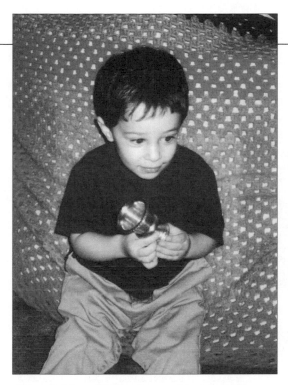

Steven holds an Elijah's Cup used by his great-grandfather, Cherie's grandfather.

Seth and Cheryl examine a kiddush cup used by their great-great-grandfather. On the cup is engraved the word "Kamenitz," the name of the town in Russia where he was born.

Family Treasures

Is there something that has been in your family for many years, like a tablecloth, *kiddush* (**kid-DOOSH** or **KID-dush**) cup, or candlesticks? Is there a family heirloom seder plate? Have some of these items been handed down from generation to generation? Ask your seder guests to bring these treasures to the seder and to tell a story about them. Remember these stories, and write them down (with drawings or photographs) in a special notebook where you preserve important facts and stories about your family and friends.

Cherie has many beautiful Passover objects from her family that she uses each year. The silver candlesticks are from her great-grandparents on her father's side. The silver and glass container for the horseradish was a gift her mother's mother received from friends who went to Israel a long time ago. The silverware belonged to her parents. And the very

Alison shows her great-grandmother's (Cherie's grandmother's) Israeli candlesticks to her friend Pearl.

little silver spoon for the horseradish is the one that Cherie was fed with when she was an infant!

Barbara's family uses a seder plate and a *matzah* plate that her husband's mother received from her parents. The plates came from London. They are made of china and have lovely paintings of the order of the Passover seder.

Barbara's matzah plate.

CRAFT

Immigration Bookmarks

Here's a way to make something that you can use at Passover—and all year long—to remind you of someone in your family who has emigrated from another country. If you do not have a particular person in mind, you can choose one country where people have emigrated from, and use it for your first bookmark. Each year, you can make a new bookmark to remind you of another immigration story.

WHAT YOU NEED:

2 pieces, each 6"x 1½", of clear plastic contact paper (see-through and sticky on one side)

paper to draw on

scissors

small, flat pictures or other items from or about the country you choose

hole puncher

piece of colored yarn, 6" long

WHAT YOU DO:

1. Decide which country to show on your bookmark.
2. Gather pictures that remind you of the country and of immigration: pictures or drawings of the flag, clothing, suitcases, ship, airplane, foods, or other items.
3. Add real things like stamps, photos, or anything else that is flat.
4. Remove the protective backing from one of the strips of contact paper and place it sticky side up on a table.
5. Arrange the items on the table next to the plastic. When you like the design, transfer them carefully onto the sticky plastic, pressing them flat.
6. Remove the backing from the other piece of contact paper, and very carefully place it directly on top of the piece with your design, making sure that the two pieces line up together to form one piece.
7. Carefully smooth out the bookmark by rubbing it from one end to the other.
8. Punch a hole at the top center of the bookmark and thread the yarn through it, making a double knot at the end to form a loop.

Enjoy your bookmark! Use it to keep your place in the *Haggadah*—or for other Passover reading.

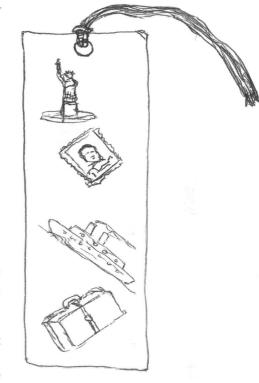

What country does this bookmark represent?
Larry Schwartz

INTRODUCTION

This drawing of the walls of Jerusalem was made in Jerusalem over a hundred years ago!
Jerusalem Haggadah, 1863

No seder would be complete without remembering Jerusalem. For thousands of years, the holy city has been in the thoughts and hearts of Jewish people, not just at their seders but all through the year. Since ancient times Jerusalem has been—and still is—the holiest of all cities for the Jewish people. Built by King David about three thousand years ago, the city was called Jerusalem, which means "City of Peace." Later, David's son, King Solomon, built the Holy Temple there, and people from all over the country came to Jerusalem to pray.

Three times a year, Jews came to Jerusalem to celebrate special holidays known as the *Shalosh Regalim, the three pilgrimage holidays, which are* Sukkot *(the fall harvest holiday),* Shavuot *(the spring harvest festival celebrated to recall the giving of the Torah), and* Pesach!

Over the centuries, Jews living outside Israel began to come to Jerusalem, individually and in small and large groups. The very syllables "Je-ru-sa-lem" became a kind of chant, a kind of prayer, representing the idea of Israel, not just the land but the people, too. The word "Jerusalem" stirred up longings in Jews all over the world to come to Israel, to live and pray in the Holy Land.

Today the only part of the original Holy Temple still standing is a portion of the Western

The Kotel—the Western Wall in Jerusalem.
Cherie Karo Schwartz

Wall. Each year millions of Jews come to pray at the Wall (in Hebrew, the "Kotel"; **KOH-tell**) in the belief that the presence of God is always there. Once a city behind walls and gates, Jerusalem is now much larger than the ancient city of David's time. It is a city holy and important to Moslems and Christians, as well as Jews, and all three peoples live there. Although many, many wars have been fought over Jerusalem, the city still stands today. In our prayers, we always pray that Jerusalem may one day again be the "City of Peace."

Barbara says: "Wherever you walk in Jerusalem, you walk in the footsteps of history: King David and King Solomon of the Bible; the Greeks, the Romans, and all the other people who came to this city. For thousands of years the stones of Jerusalem have listened to all those people, and, if the stones could talk, they would tell many stories."

In this chapter you'll discover ways to link yourself with Jerusalem and with Israel.

WHO LIVES IN JERUSALEM?
IN 1998:
423,600 JEWS
168,000 MOSLEMS
13,600 CHRISTIANS
2,600 PEOPLE OF OTHER
    RELIGIONS
TOTAL: 607,800 PEOPLE

STORY

Fifteen years ago, when Barbara lived in Jerusalem, she was inspired to write this story.

Jerusalem's Secret

Jerusalem is filled with magic!

It is an earthly city, where people of all faiths walk and work together in the hustle and bustle of everyday life. But it is a city of the spirit, too, where three great peoples—Christians, Moslems, and Jews—share faith and history, art and architecture, music and dance, food and ways of dress. The very sounds and smells of the city's different faiths give it a special magic not found anywhere else on earth.

O. J. Mechanic, age 9

Now, I would like to tell you a secret. When you go to Jerusalem, you too may feel the magic of the city. Every part of your body—from the tips of your toes to the top of your head—may come to know the secrets, the mysteries, the special charms of Jerusalem. Are you interested? But I warn you: there is a price to pay. Are you still interested?

Kindergarten children from the Jewish Community Day School of Durham, N.C., create Jerusalem on a felt wall-hanging.

O.J. Mechanic, age 9

You see, there are many gates into the city of Jerusalem. You may enter the city through any one of those gates, except, of course, the Gate of Mercy, which is closed until the coming of the Messiah. So, according to legend, you may enter Jerusalem through any one of her open gates, but if you want to learn the special secrets of the city, you must give your heart to the gatekeeper. Then, as you walk the streets of the city, the legend says, as you inhale the city's fragrances and listen to its sounds, as you step in the footsteps of its history, the gatekeeper will keep your heart. And then, when you are ready to leave the city, to go back to the place from which you have come, the gatekeeper will return your heart.

That seems simple enough, doesn't it? But, remember, there's a price to pay! When you leave the city, the gatekeeper will keep one little piece of your heart with him in Jerusalem. So, no matter where you go on the face of the earth, no matter how hard you try to forget the city, that little piece of your heart still with the gatekeeper will call you to come back, to return to Jerusalem.

FUN

Israeli Pen Pals

Would you like to write to young people in Israel? You could share news, stories, and hobbies.

And think of all the Israeli stamps you could get for your collection! How can you find someone to write to? Look in your local Jewish newspaper or ask at your synagogue. If you have access to a computer and the Internet, you can log-on to www.epals.com and search for Hebrew-speaking students in Israel.

A Bar/Bat Mitzvah Trip to Israel

If you're ready to become a Bar or Bat Mitzvah, you may want to celebrate this important occasion with your family at the Western Wall in Jerusalem, then spend some time visiting the rest of Israel. Some companies offer special reduced fares for the Bar/Bat Mitzvah! If you would like information on the special programs available, look in Jewish magazines or newspapers, contact your synagogue, Central Agency, or Bureau of Jewish Education, or call or write directly to:

UJA Federations of North America,
 National Missions Department,
111 Eighth Avenue,
Suite 11E, New York, NY
10011-5201
Phone: 212-284-6519.
 Fax: 212-284-6836.

Plan an Israel Exhibit

"The walls of Jerusalem, the city where I live."
Yoni Dinur, age 13

Here's an idea: If you can't go to Israel, why not "bring" Israel to your town or community? There are many places in your community where you could create an Israel exhibit—your synagogue, Jewish day school, Jewish museum, Jewish Community Center (JCC), or even the public library.

People who have been to Israel will probably be delighted to lend pictures, photographs, maps, and other interesting objects that they've brought home from Jerusalem and Israel. Ask people in your community to lend you these items. Students in religious schools can create drawings, collages, and poems to go with the exhibit. Set up your exhibit in a wide hallway, and invite people to come for a very special program. You might even ask people to talk about their memories of Israel, especially if they visited Israel a long time ago or were there before 1948, before Israel became a state. Think about making a com-

munity "Israel memories" album with photographs and stories. It's a terrific opportunity to "visit" Israel without leaving home!

CRAFTS

A Jerusalem Puzzle

WHAT YOU NEED:

magazines, post cards, colored paper, travel brochures
scissors
all-purpose paste
magic markers
heavy construction paper or thin poster board

WHAT YOU DO:

1. Cut pictures of Jerusalem and Israel from magazines, travel brochures, and picture post cards.
2. Write a few sentences about Jerusalem on colored paper. These can be lines from poetry or songs, or you can create them, like:

   "Each new day in Jerusalem has a promise of peace."

   "Jerusalem is a weaving of many peoples, colors, sights, and sounds."
3. Paste the cut-out pictures and words on a piece of light-weight poster board or heavy construction paper.
4. After the paste has dried, cut the picture into jigsaw pieces.
5. Put all the pieces in an envelope.
6. Enjoy putting your puzzle together!

   HELPFUL HINT: If you make more than one puzzle, label the back of each piece of the same puzzle and its envelope with the same number. In case some pieces get misplaced, you will know which envelope to put them back into again.

A Papercut Mizrach

When Jews pray, it's traditional to face Jerusalem, the city of the Holy Temple. If you ever wondered why so many Jews (in the western world) face east while they pray, now you know—Jerusalem is to the east!

In many Jewish homes, a special plaque or picture is hung on the eastern wall. It's called a *mizrach* (**mizz-RACH** or **MIZZ-rach**), the

Hebrew word for east, and reminds us of the direction of Jerusalem. It also adds the holiness of Jerusalem to our homes. For hundreds of years, Jews have been creating beautiful *mizrachim* (plural of *mizrach*) for their homes and synagogues.

A favorite kind of *mizrach* is made by cutting designs into paper, called paper cutting. You can make this kind of *mizrach,* too, just as Jews have done for many, many generations.

WHAT YOU NEED:

scrap paper 8½" x 11"
a piece of white paper 8½" x 11"
a piece of dark colored paper (like black, blue, green, purple) 8½" x 11"
pointed scissors
pencil
glue
fine-point magic markers (choose from gold, blue, or any other colors you like)

Freya Mechanic

WHAT YOU DO:

1. On scratch paper, draw an outline of the buildings in the Old City of Jerusalem. Include the building tops, domes, and towers. Use pictures and drawings of Jerusalem to help you decide what Jerusalem looks like.

2. Draw cut-outs for windows and doorways.

3. Now trace your outline on the white sheet of paper, cut it out, and carefully make the cut-outs.

4. Glue the white paper design onto the dark sheet of paper so that the dark color shows through.

5. Many artists who make papercuts write on the papercut with gold or colored ink. You can do this, too. With the fine-tipped magic markers, write a saying about Jerusalem. Choose a saying from the Bible, like:

> "Pray for the peace of Jerusalem.
> May those who love You be at peace." (Psalm 122:6–7)

or from the *Haggadah,* like:

"Next year in Jerusalem!"

or, create your own phrase in Hebrew or English.

6. Hang your *mizrach* on the eastern wall of your home.

SEDER TALK
Next Year in Jerusalem

At the end of the seder we say, "Next year in Jerusalem!" or, in Hebrew, "*L'shanah Ha'ba'ah B'Yerushalayim.*" In Israel people say, "Next year in Jerusalem rebuilt." What does this mean? Do you think the Temple really should be rebuilt? Exactly the way it was? What should be the same? What should be different?

PROJECT
A Prayer for Jerusalem

"Next year in Jerusalem!" printed on a German hand towel.
Germany, late 1800s

What is the place of Jerusalem in our hearts?

What does it mean to long to return to Israel?

What are some ways that we can return?

People from all over the world pray in their hearts for peace in Jerusalem and Israel. Here is the beautiful prayer of the Israeli peace poet, Dr. Ada Aharoni:

"I arrived in Israel when Israel was just two years old (1950). She became my own special baby, whom I had to care for and love. I took her in my arms, and planted my roots deeply in her soil, and she bore wonderful fruit and blossomed like an almond tree in full bloom. I have been in Israel for forty-five years now, and my foremost wish is to see this blooming tree flourishing in a Middle East of peace and harmony, and good relations with all our neighbors, as it was in the past, and may still be in the present and future. Amen . . . may it be. . . ."

Many times over thousands of years, Jerusalem has been attacked and nearly destroyed, but the city still survives. Yet the "City of Peace" is still not at peace. In the Psalms of King David, we read, "Pray for the peace of Jerusalem."

Geismar Haggadah, Germany, 1928

What are some prayers that we can offer for Jerusalem?

Ask your seder guests to create a poem together. Each person may add one line:

"Oh, Jerusalem, we wish for you . . ."

Can you write your own prayer for peace?

SONG

There are many melodies for "Next Year in Jerusalem." Sing your favorite melody with your seder guests. Here is one of our favorites.

NEXT YEAR IN JERUSALEM!
L'-shanah haba'ah bi-ru-sha-la-yim

לְשָׁנָה הַבָּאָה בִּירוּשָׁלָיִם.

INTRODUCTION

The seder's conclusion is joyful and full of song. We sing the same songs that Jews have sung for hundreds of years, songs that praise and tell the greatness of God. We also look to the future, and we talk about our hopes for the next year. As you sing these songs, bringing this year's seder to a close, ask yourself what you can do from this Passover to the next year that will make a difference to yourself, your family, and your community.

SONGS

"*Adir Hu*" means "God is mighty." This song is hundreds of years old. In fact, the first time that "*Adir Hu*" appeared in a *Haggadah* was in the fourteenth century in Germany. Each line of the song begins with a different letter of the Hebrew alphabet. "How blessed is God in all the world and may the Holy Temple be rebuilt soon."

Judy Lande Haran

Ending with Praises and Songs

Adir Hu

Traditional

A - dir hu a - dir hu yiv - ne ve - to b' - ka - rov

bim - hc - ra____ bim - hc - ra b' - ya - mc - nu b' - ka - rov

El b' - ne El b' - ne b' - ne vet - cha b' - ka - rov

Mighty are You! May You rebuild Your house
    soon,
Speedily, speedily, in our days, soon!
O God, rebuild, O God rebuild, rebuild Your
    house soon!

אַדִּיר הוּא. יִבְנֶה בֵיתוֹ בְּקָרוֹב.

בִּמְהֵרָה. בִּמְהֵרָה. בְּיָמֵינוּ בְּקָרוֹב.

אֵל בְּנֵה. אֵל בְּנֵה. בְּנֵה בֵיתְךָ בְּקָרוֹב:

The next song is called "Who knows One" in English. It has thirteen verses, each one starting with the words "Who knows . . ." and adding the numbers one to thirteen, with each verse linking the number with something important in Judaism, such as the number five and the Five Books of Moses, or ten and the Ten Commandments, or twelve and the Twelve Tribes of Israel. The refrain, which is sung after each verse, reminds us there is only *one* God. In many families, the song is sung faster and faster with each verse to see who can finish singing all the verses first. When the song is sung in Ladino, it is called "Quen Supiese" ("Who Would Know"). Here is the last verse as translated from both the Ashkenazic and Sephardic versions:

"Who knows the answer to one? I know the answer to one: One is our God in Heaven and Earth, two are the Tablets, three are the Patriarchs, four are the Matriarchs, five are the Books of Moses, six are the volumes of Mishnah, seven are the days of the week, eight are the days of the covenant, nine are the months to childbirth, ten are the Commandments, eleven are the stars in Joseph's dream, twelve are the tribes of Israel, and thirteen are the attributes of God."

Judy Lande Haran

Eḥad Mi Yodei-a

Allegretto

Who knows one? I know one.
One is our God, in heaven and on earth.

Who knows two? I know two.
Two are the tablets of the covenant;
One is our God, in heaven and on earth.

אֶחָד מִי יוֹדֵעַ אֶחָד אֲנִי יוֹדֵעַ
אֶחָד אֱלֹהֵינוּ שֶׁבַּשָּׁמַיִם וּבָאָרֶץ

שְׁנַיִם מִי יוֹדֵעַ שְׁנַיִם אֲנִי יוֹדֵעַ
שְׁנֵי לֻחוֹת הַבְּרִית
אֶחָד אֱלֹהֵינוּ שֶׁבַּשָּׁמַיִם וּבָאָרֶץ

Quen Supiese

Allegretto

Ladino folktune

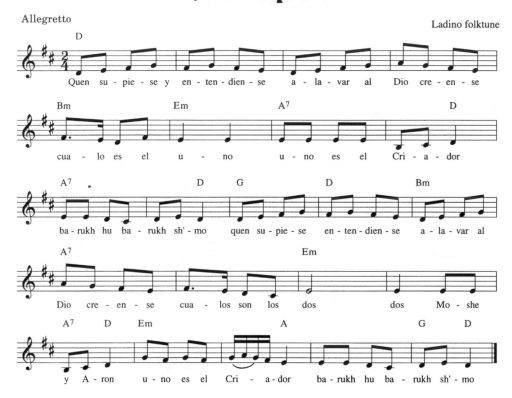

Quen su - pie - se y en - ten - dien - se a - la - var al Dio cre - en - se

cua - lo es el u - no u - no es el Cri - a - dor

ba - rukh hu ba - rukh sh' - mo quen su - pie - se en - ten - dien - se a - la - var al

Dio cre - en - se cua - los son los dos dos Mo - she

y A - ron u - no es el Cri - a - dor ba - rukh hu ba - rukh sh' - mo

Who would know and understand, praising and believing in God?

What is one alone? One is the Creator, Blessed be He, blessed be His name.

What are two? Two are Moses and Aaron; One is the Creator, Blessed be He, blessed be His name.

What are three? Three are our fathers: Abraham, Isaac, Jacob; Two Moses and Aaron, One is the Creator, etc...

What are four? Four are our mother: Sarah, Rivka, Leah, Rachel, Three are our fathers, etc...

What are five? Five books of the Law, etc...

What are six? Six days of the week, etc...

What are seven? Seven days with the Sabbath, etc...

What are eight? Eight days for the circumcision, etc...

What are nine? Nine months of pregnancy, etc...

What are ten? Ten commandments of the Law, etc...

What are eleven? Eleven tribes without Joseph, etc...

What are twelve? Twelve tribes with Joseph, etc...

Quen supiese y entendiese, alavar al Dio creense cualo es el uno:

Uno es el Criador, Baruch hu, baruch sh'mo

Quen supiese y entendiese alavar al Dio creense

Cualos son los dos: Dos Moshe y Aron, Uno es el Criador, Baruch hu baruch sh'mo

Cualos son los tres: tres padres muestros son: Avram Yitzchak, Yaakov, Dos Moshe.........

Cualos son los cuatro: Cuatro madres muestras son:, Sara, Rivka, Leah, Rachel, Tres muestros padres.....,

Cualos son los cinco-cinco livros de la Ley etc.....,

Cualos son los seij-seij dias de la semana, cinco etc.....,

Cualos son los siete-siete dias con Shabbat, seij etc....,

Cualos son los ocho-ocho dias de la mila, siete etc..,

Cualos son mueve-mueve mezes de la prenada, etc.,

Cualos son los diez-diez mandamientos de la Ley, etc,

Cualos son los onze-onze trivos sin Yosef, diez, etc...,

Cualos son los doze-doze trivos con Yosef, onze, etc..

Eisenstein Haggadah, U.S., 1928: illustration by Lola

Jews all over the world have been singing *"Chad Gadya,"* a song-story, for more than five hundred years. People in different places sing the song to different melodies. This melody is sung by many Ashkenazic Jews in the United States.

One little goat, my father bought for two coins.
Then came a cat and ate the goat my father bought
for two coins. Then came a dog and bit the cat that
ate the goat my father bought for two coins........

חַד גַּדְיָא חַד גַּדְיָא
דְּזַבִּין אַבָּא בִּתְרֵי זוּזֵי
חַד גַּדְיָא חַד גַּדְיָא

וְאָתָא שׁוּנְרָא וְאָכְלָה לְגַדְיָא
דְּזַבִּין אַבָּא בִּתְרֵי זוּזֵי
חַד גַּדְיָא חַד גַּדְיָא

Ishayah and Shoshanah pet their own Chad Gadya.

Can you read the words below? Do you know what they say?

Un Cavritico
Y vino el Santo Bendicho El y mato al malakh hamavet
Ki se yevo al shohet
Ke mato al buey
Ke se bevio el agua
Ke amato al fuego
Ke kemo al palo
Ke aharvo al perro
Ke mordio al gato
Ke comio al cavritico
Ke lo merco mi padre
Por dos levanim, por dos levanim.

Budapest Haggadah, Hungary, 20th century

This is the last verse of "*Chad Gadya*" in Ladino, a language spoken by Jews in Spain and Portugal and other parts of southern Europe (whose ancestors had traveled there from Spain at the end of the 1400s). Sometimes it is called Judeo-Spanish or Judeo-Español. The words are a mixture of Spanish and Hebrew, and may be written in Hebrew or in the same alphabet letters that we use. Jews from different countries sing "*Chad Gadya*" in different languages: Yiddish, Aramaic, Ladino, and also the spoken languages of the country where they live.

"*Chad Gadya*" tells the story of what happened to the kid (baby goat) that Father bought for two *zuzim* (**ZOO-zeem**) (coins). It may be a story about a little goat, and it may also be a story about Jewish history. The goat may be the Holy Temple. (King David is said to have paid two *zuzim* for each tribe of Israel.)

The cat eats the goat (cat = King of Assyria, who conquered the Jews), the dog bites the cat (dog = Babylonian King Nebuchadnezzar [**Neh-bu-chad-NEHZ-er**], who conquered the Assyrians), the stick beats the dog (stick = the Persians who conquered the Babylonians), the fire

burns the stick (fire = the Greek King Alexander the Great, who conquered the Persians), the water puts out the fire (water = the Jewish Maccabees, who conquered the Seleucids [**seh-LOO-sydz**], who came from the Greeks), the ox drinks the water (ox = the Romans, who conquered the Maccabees), the butcher kills the ox (butcher = the Moslems who conquered the Romans), the Angel of Death kills the butcher (Angel of Death = the European nations), and then the Holy One kills the Angel of Death.

God is the most powerful of all.

Eisenstein Haggadah, U.S., 1920s: illustration by Lola

CRAFT

A Chad Gadya Glove

There are ten characters in the *Chad Gadya* story. You can make a pair of gloves with ten fingers, and tell the story of "*Chad Gadya*" while you sing the song.

WHAT YOU NEED:

a pair of lightweight garden gloves
colored fine magic markers

WHAT YOU DO:

1. Set the gloves out on a table with the inside of the "hands," the "palms," facing up.
2. Starting with one "thumb" of one of the gloves, draw a face on each finger, in order of the lines of the song.
3. When you have finished drawing the faces, you can wear both gloves, or you can wear one glove and let someone else wear the other glove.
4. While the seder guests sing the *"Chad Gadya"* song, as each character is mentioned, make that finger character dance and wiggle.

ANOTHER IDEA: If you like, instead of drawing on the glove, put a small piece of Velcro onto each finger. Make the *Chad Gadya* characters out of felt, attach a piece of Velcro to the back of each, and stick the characters onto the fingers of the glove.

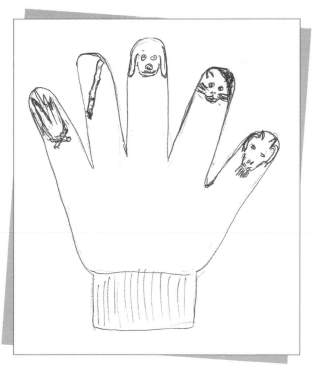

Larry Schwartz

First, hold the matzo under running water.

CUSTOMS

Happy Passover

Before Passover, Jews in parts of France and Germany greet each other with a special Passover greeting. Instead of saying, "Happy Passover," they say, "May you have a good building." This greeting, like the words of the song *"Adir Hu,"* are a way of saying, "May the Temple be rebuilt soon."

After the Seder

Whew! What a holiday! It's hard to believe the Passover seder is finished. How sad it is to say goodbye to friends and family—and to the lovely spirit of the seder! But there are many days of Passover left and many ways to celebrate. Here are four ways Jews around the world celebrate Passover after the seder ends.

1. Beating the Water

Descendants of the "Secret Jews" of Spain and Portugal go to a stream and beat the water with willow branches. This is a reminder of how the waters of the Reed Sea were parted so that the Children of Israel could cross to freedom.

2. More Matzo

Even though there are many foods forbidden on Passover, there are many wonderful foods that we *may* eat, especially foods made with—you guessed it—*matzo!* A favorite Ashkenazic Passover breakfast meal is *matzo brei*—*matzo* held under running water to soften, then mixed in with beaten eggs, and fried in a small amount of butter. It's delicious served with jam or cinnamon sugar! It tastes like French toast! Yummmmm!

3. Visiting Friends

On the evening of the last day of Passover, many Sephardic and Oriental Jews go in groups from house to house, bidding farewell to the *Pesach* holiday and wishing each other a happy year. Moroccan Jews eat from a special table as they go from house to house. On the table are scattered green leaves, plates of green candies, and cakes. Can you guess why there is so much green on the table? Remember, just like the *karpas* on the seder plate, green is a color of rebirth in the spring.

4. Maimuna (My-MOO-nah)

On the day after *Pesach*, Moroccan Jews in Israel hold a gigantic party called *Maimuna*. People from all over Israel gather in a park, wearing colorful embroidered clothes, and listen to bands playing festive music. Children play games. Everyone shares delicious foods, such as pancakes called *muflita*, buttermilk, figs, and sweet desserts. The mood is happy and joyous. Jews in North America have started having *Maimuna* celebrations, too.

SEDER TALK

Ending the Seder

What happens at the end of your seder? Wouldn't it be great to have a very special way to end your family's seder and to have it become your family's tradition every year? How do you want your seder to end? Do people just leave the table to stretch their legs and clean away the many dishes? You might say, "*L'hitraot*" (**le-HIT-rah-ot**), which is Hebrew for "so long until we meet again!" Or hug each other. Or you might ask, "Who wants to help with the dishes and *shlep* (Yiddish for drag) all the chairs back?" (Just kidding!)

Or you might sing some or all of the songs in this chapter, or "*Lo Yisa Goy,*" a song that some people in Israel sing at the end of the seder. It is a song of peace from the Bible (in Isaiah 2:4). The words in Hebrew say:

"Nation shall not lift up sword against nation,
Neither shall they learn war any more."

A Moroccan dress for Maimuna.
Lucy Schwartz, age 15

Lo Yisa Goy

Folk Song

Lo yi-sa goy el goy che-rev____ lo yil-m'-du od mil-cha-

mah____ lo yi-sa goy el goy che-rev____ lo yil-m'-du od mil-cha-

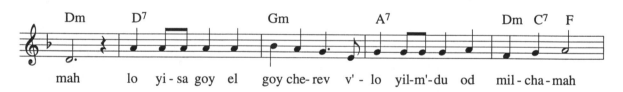

mah lo yi-sa goy el goy che-rev v'-lo yil-m'-du od mil-cha-mah

lo yi-sa goy el goy che-rev v'-lo yil-m'-du od mil-cha-mah

Nation shall not lift up sword against nation,
neither shall they study war anymore

לֹא־יִשָּׂא גוֹי
אֶל־גּוֹי חֶרֶב
וְלֹא־יִלְמְדוּ עוֹד
מִלְחָמָה

There are many melodies to this song. Sing your favorite one with your seder guests, or find a song that is about freedom, spring, or hope that everyone can learn and sing together. Here are four ideas to help you create your very own new tradition:

- Find a beautiful poem about family, being together, or Passover that you can read aloud together, or take turns reading.
- Hold hands around the seder table and say a special goodbye to each other.
- Give each person a tiny piece of the *afikoman* to take home as a reminder of the seder, and to bring good luck.
- You have all planted the seeds of new ideas at the seder, so now you can give flower, herb, or vegetable seeds to each guest to take home and plant for the spring.

A FINAL SEDER QUESTION

How Can We Make a Good Start for the Next Year?

Passover is celebrated in the month of *Nisan,* the first month in the Hebrew calendar. It is a holiday of freedom and new beginnings, so it is an excellent time to make new beginnings for yourself, your family, and your friends. What can *you* do? Take a minute at the end of your seder to think about this:

- Is there something you do that you wish you could do differently or better?

    Make a fresh start at changing it.

- Is there a project that your family wanted to do all winter but never got around to?

    Make a new start on getting it done.

- Is there someone you have had trouble getting along with?

    Make a new beginning with that person.

- Is there someone or some group or organization that could use your help?

    Find out, and make a new start at volunteering.

FUN

A Last Detective Test

Now that you have learned so very much about the Passover holiday and celebrations, can you find all of these Passover words in this puzzle?

WINE

MAROR

CHAROSES

EGG

BONE

SALTWATER

MOSES

AARON

PARSLEY

PHARAOH

MIRIAM

HAGGADAH

PESACH

ELIJAH

AFIKOMAN

```
Z P X Y M A R P H Z H K W A S I
H R Z Q P J D A O V A C K A A I
B A D A F R Z D A Q G A G K L M
N Z Z Q Z O X P R H G A R R T Z
K A D T D R O M A X A Y Y P W Z
A P Z B A A K I H M D I E L A G
H E Z R Q M P P P P A O G L T K
J S I G A H H K Z L H J G F E A
H A R E V O S S A P S O I A R M
G C K R I M Q G I E L Z K R E Z
P H Q E L I J A H A N M O E M O
L S K J H E R W N I L O Z M P A
M A A R O N H I A H F Z B K M K
Z P S D G O F N Y E L S R A P Z
A H I L S B K E M A I R I M I A
Q C H A R O S E S Z I Q F E P P
L N A M O K I F A H M O S E S A
```

Seth Rush, age 9

May the days from this Passover to the next be filled with many blessings, sweet surprises, and good stories for you, your family, your friends, and your community. Happy Passover!

Mira, who speaks Yiddish, wishes you "A Sweet Passover."

YOUR IDEAS FOR YOUR NEXT SEDER!

Throughout this book, you have learned many old and new ways to celebrate Passover. Now it is your turn to create new ideas for your next year's seder. And what better time to record your ideas than right now!

Here is a blank page for you to write down your favorite new ideas for stories, activities, games, foods, crafts, and songs. Then, when you open your book next year, you will be ready to create another new and beautiful celebration of Passover!

P.S. To learn more about Passover, turn the page...

More about Passover
Fun-filled Books, Tapes, and Videos

Books to Read

Books about the Exodus Story and Passover Celebration

Chaiken, Miriam. *Ask Another Question: The Story and Meaning of Passover*. New York: Clarion, 1985. Tells the history and importance of Passover.

Fishman, Cathy Goldberg. *On Passover*. New York: Atheneum, 1997. A young girl follows her senses: seeing, tasting, feeling, smelling to find the meaning of Passover.

Fluek, Toby Knobel, with Lillian Fluek Finkler. *Passover As I Remember It*. New York: Alfred A. Knopf, 1994. A personal Passover remembrance of her childhood in a small *shtetl*.

Goldin, Barbara Diamond. *The Passover Journey: A Seder Companion*. New York: Viking, 1994. A retelling of the Exodus story plus seder traditions.

——— with illustrations by Neil Waldman. *The Passover Journey—A Seder Companion*. New York: Viking Childrens Books, 1994. A lushly illustrated companion to each aspect of the Passover seder and story, rituals, and traditions.

Hirsh, Marilyn. *I Love Passover*. New York: Holiday House, 1985. An introduction to Passover for little children.

Lepon, Shoshana. *The Ten Plagues of Egypt*. Brooklyn: The Judaica Press, 1988. A humorous poem about the Ten Plagues.

Marcus, Audrey Friedman and Raymond A. Zwerin. *But This Night Is Different*. New York: UAHC, 1980. A presentation of how Passover is different than other days.

Schwartz, Lynne Sharon. *The Four Questions*. New York: Dial Press, 1989. The Four Questions are presented with beautiful, colorful illustrations by Ori Sherman.

Simon, Norma. *The Story of Passover*. New York: HarperCollins, 1993. The story of the Exodus plus ideas for celebrating the seder.

Teutsch, Betsy Platkin. *One Little Goat—Had Gadya*. New York: Jason Aronson, 1990. Beautifully illustrated story that the cumulative song tells.

Books to Share with Little Children

Auerbach, Julie Jaslow. *Everything is Changing: It's Pesach*. Rockville, Md.: Kar-Ben Copies, 1986. A rhyming story of all the things that are different on Passover.

Gikow, Louise. *Kippi and the Missing Matzah: A Sesame Street Passover*. New York: Comet International, 1994. A fun book about Kippi, who comes from Israel to make a seder for his Sesame Street friends.

Kimmelman, Leslie. *Hooray! It's Passover!* New York: HarperCollins, 1996. A family celebrates the seder and tells the Exodus story.

Miller, Deborah Uchill. *Only Nine Chairs*. Rockville, Md.: Kar-Ben Copies, 1982. A funny story about how to fit nineteen seder guests into nine chairs.

Winkler, Madeline. *Let's Have a Seder!* Rockville, Md.: Kar-Ben Copies, 1997. A board book showing animals and children at their first seder. For toddlers and nursery school children.

Zilfert, Harriet. *What Is Passover?* New York: HarperCollins, 1995. Lift the flaps to find out about Passover traditions.

Passover Stories

Atlas, Susan. *The Passover Passage*. Los Angeles: Torah Aura, 1989. A family on a sailboat in the Caribbean during Passover learns more about freedom.

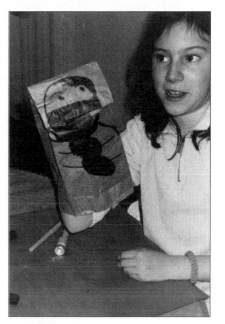

Bat-Ami, Miriam. *Dear Elijah*. Philadelphia: The Jewish Publication Society, 1997. When a girl's father is hospitalized and can't attend the family seder, she decides to write to Elijah the Prophet. For older elementary school readers.

Cohen, Barbara. *The Carp in the Bathtub*. Rockville, Md.: Kar-Ben Copies, 1972. The humorous story of two children who try to save the life of a fish being kept alive until Passover. For middle elementary school readers.

Feder, Harriet K. *Not Yet Elijah*. Rockville, Md.: Kar-Ben Copies, 1988. A rhymed story about Elijah's visit to a seder.

Fluek, Toby, with Lillian Fluek Finkler. *Passover as I Remember It*. New York: Alfred A. Knopf, 1994. The description of Passover preparations in prewar Poland. For older elementary school and junior high readers.

Goldin, Barbara Diamond. *The Magician's Visit*. New York: Puffin Books, 1993. A retelling of the Yiddish story by I. L. Peretz, about how Elijah the Prophet helps a poor couple who want to celebrate Passover.

Heymsfeld, Carla. *The Matzah Ball Fairy*. New York: UAHC, 1996. A fairy pops out of a cooking *matzah* ball and offers special magic to the cooking and to the entire seder.

Kessler, Brad. *Moses in Egypt*. New York: Simon and Schuster, 1997. The Exodus story told for all, simply and well, with a background of subtly-colored, strongly evocative illustrations.

Manushkin, Fran. *Miriam's Cup: A Passover Story*. New York: Scholastic Press, 1998. A girl named Miriam receives a special Passover gift: a Cup of Miriam for her family's seder table, complete with the story of the biblical Miriam.

———.*The Matzah That Papa Brought Home*. New York: Scholastic, Inc., 1995. A cumulative song with beautiful illustrations.

Medoff, Francine. *The Mouse in the Matzah Factory*. Rockville, Md.: Kar-Ben

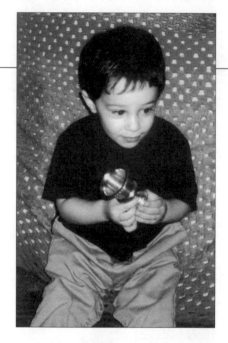

Copies, 1983. A mouse from a wheat field makes his way to a *matzah* factory and watches how *matzah* is made.

Newman, Leslea. *Matzoh Ball Moon*. New York: Clarion, 1998. A grandmother and granddaughter make delicious *matzoh* balls and other foods.

Portnoy, Mindy Avra. *The Matzah Ball*. Rockville, Md.: Kar-Ben Copies, 1997. A boy's special Passover food at the baseball game saves the day.

Schilder, Rosalind. *Dayenu or How Uncle Murray Saved the* Seder. Rockville, Md.: Kar-Ben Copies, 1988. A couple tricks themselves into making the seder.

Schotter, Roni. *Passover Magic*. Boston: Little Brown, 1995. A magician uncle hides the family's *afikoman*.

Schwartz, Howard. *Miriam's Tambourine: Jewish Folktales From Around the World*. New York: Oxford University Press, 1986. This book includes a folktale from Eastern Europe about the tambourine.

Waldon, Kathleen Cook. *A Wilderness Passover*. Red Deer, Alberta, Canada: Northern Lights Books for Children, 1994. A family at an isolated lake learns more about the spirit of Passover.

Wohl, Lauren N. *Matzoh Mouse*. New York: HarperCollins, 1991. A little girl cannot resist opening the chocolate-covered *matzoh*. The family looks for the "*matzoh* mouse" who has eaten it.

Zusman, Evelyn. *The Passover Parrot*. Rockville, Md.: Kar-Ben Copies, 1983. A parrot joins the family, learns to recite "*mah nishtanah*," and becomes involved with the family's seder.

Passover Fun Books

Poskanzer, Susan Cornell. *What Can It Be?* Parsippany, N.J.: Silver Press, 1991. Discover Passover by answering the riddles.

Zwebner, Janet, illustrator. *Uh! Oh! Hidden Passover Objects You'll (Almost) Never Find—with Haggadah*. New York: Yellow Brick Road Press, 1994. The reader's task is to find Passover objects that are hidden in pictures.

Art Books

Kahn, Katherine. *Passover Fun: For Little Hands*. Rockville, Md.: Kar-Ben Copies, 1991. Passover projects for children to make.

Parnes, Stephen O. *The Art of Passover*. New York: Simon and Schuster, 1997. Passover art and objects show Jewish life from the Middle Ages to the present. Photos of *Haggadot,* Elijah cups, and more.

Books about Jerusalem

Kuskin, Carla. *Jerusalem, Shining Still*. New York: Harper and Row, 1987. The history of Jerusalem, shown with beautiful woodcuts.

Paris, Alan. *Jerusalem 3000: Kids Discover the City of Gold*. New York: Pitspopanny, 1995. A discovery tour through the city of Jerusalem.

Schwartz, Howard. *Next Year in Jerusalem: 3000 Years of Jewish Stories.* New York: Viking, 1996. Ancient stories of Jerusalem retold in beautiful new renditions.

Worlf, Bernard. *If I Forget Thee O Jerusalem.* New York: Dutton, 1998. Beautiful photographs of Jerusalem and its people.

Yolen, Jane. *O Jerusalem.* New York: The Blue Sky Press, 1996. Poetry and other writings about Jerusalem give a feel of the city.

Cookbooks

Friedland, Susan R. *The Passover Table.* New York: HarperCollins, 1994. Recipes of many Jewish communities. Good food for the seder and for all of Passover week.

Hankin, Gail A. *Passover Lite Kosher Cookbook.* New York: Pelican, 1996. Recipes show how to use natural and fresh ingredients in traditional Passover cooking.

Kdoshim, Jenny and Debbie Bevans. *Matzo 101.* The authors self-published this book in 1995. It contains more than one hundred recipes for using *matzah,* including lasagna and desserts, and can be ordered by calling (909) 989-4244.

Rousso, Nira. *The Passover Gourmet.* New York: Adama Books, 1987. A cookbook from Israel, with recipes from different Jewish communities for the seder and for Passover week. Beautiful photos of the foods will make you want to start cooking.

Shulman, Zell. *Let My People Eat! Passover Seders Made Simple.* New York: Macmillan, 1998. A cookbook and more, this book includes ritual foods, diverse menus, ideas for seders.

Haggadot

Bogot, Howard I. and Robert J. Orkand. *A Children's Haggadah.* New York: Central Conference of American Rabbis, 1993. A short *Haggadah,* easy for children to use.

Donahue, Shari Faden. *My Favorite Family Haggadah.* Rhinebeck, N.Y.: Mazoh and Co., 1994.

Olitsky, Rabbi Kerry M. and Rabbi Ronald H. Isaacs. *The Discovery Haggadah.* Hoboken, N.J.: Ktav, 1992.

Oren, Rony. *The Animated Haggadah.* New York: Scopus, 1989. A *Haggadah* created with clay figures.

Pliskin, Jacqueline J. *My Animated Haggadah and Story of Passover.* New York: Shapolsky, 1991.

Scharfstein, Sol. *My First Passover Haggadah.* Hoboken, N.J.: Ktav, 1986.

Segal, Eliezer Lorne. *Uncle Eli's Passover Haggadah.* San Francisco: No Starch Press, 1999. Passover fun in clever rhymes and pictures.

Silberman, Shoshana. *A Family Haggadah.* Rockville, Md.: Kar-Ben Copies,

1987. A *Haggadah* for the entire family with songs, games, and ideas for family participation.

———. *A Family Haggadah II*. Rockville, Md.: Kar-Ben Copies, 1997. Includes discussions for older children and a complete *"Birkat Hamazon"* for blessings after the meal.

Zion, Noam and David Dishon. *The Family Participation Haggadah: A Different Night*. Jerusalem, Israel: The Shalom Hartman Institute, 1997. Also available: *Leader's Guide to a Different Night*. A comprehensive, colorful *Haggadah* and more: meanings of the Four Cups, ecology of the plagues, historic *Haggadah* illustrations, family-oriented discussion questions.

Audio Tapes

The world's largest distributor of Jewish Music is Tara Publications. They have every kind and style of music from all around the world and for all holidays and occasions. Contact them at 1-800-TARA-400; or on the Net at http:/www.tara.com or http://www.jewishmusic.com. You can see and hear their offerings.

Avni, Fran. *Mostly Matzoh,* 1982. Creative, original songs, rhythms, and story by the writer of three songs in this book! Other children's recordings include: *Latkes and Hamentaschen, The Seventh Day, Israel Song Favorites,* and *Daisies and Ducklings*. For ordering these (and many adult recordings), please contact Fran at: 4841 Isabella, Montreal, Quebec H3W1S6 CANADA, or Tara Publications (see above).

Celebrate With Us: Passover. Jewish Family Productions, 1989. For children and family; teaches about the holiday and things to think about.

Friedman, Debbie. *Let's Celebrate: Passover*. Behrman House, 1987. Entertaining and delightful songs by Debbie Friedman.

Gaon, Yehoram. *Passover in the Sephardic Tradition*. CBS Records, Israel, n.d. Music and songs, Hebrew and Ladino, Sephardic and Oriental.

Hirschhorn, Linda, with Vocolot. *Gather Round*. It includes "Miriam's Slow Snake Dance," which is in this book! For information on other Vocolot recordings, please contact Linda at: 424 North Street, Oakland, Ca., 94609 or Tara Publications.

Klezmer Conservatory Band (with Theodore Bikel). *A Taste of Passover*. Rounder Records, 1998. From Yiddish to Hebrew to Ladino; a broad variety of story and song.

Paley, Cindy. *A Singing* Seder. CPL, 1995. Contemporary and traditional songs; includes lyrics in transliteration.

Parchi, Chaim. *Haggadah Songs*. CP Music, 1986. Beautifully sung Ashkenazic, Sephardic, and original songs for the seder.

Politzer, Cantor David. *The Passover Celebration: Songs for the Seder Meal*. LTP Cassettes, 1980.

Schwartz, Cherie Karo. *Cherie Karo Schwartz Tells Passover Stories From Kar-Ben Copies.* Kar-Ben Copies, Inc., 1987. The author of this Passover book (and *My Lucky Dreidel*) reads Passover stories.

Voice of the Turtle. *A Different Night: A Passover Musical Anthology.* Kol HaTor, 1996. Medieval and ancient Middle Eastern music, including twenty-three worldwide versions of *"Chad Gadya."*

Zim, Paul. *Passover Seder Sing-A-Sing and Seder Nights.* Simcha, 1996. A children's chorus joins the singer on traditional melodies.

Zim, Sol. *Family Seder: A Passover Sing-a-Long for the Entire Family.* Zimray Enterprises, 1979. Old traditional tunes with contemporary sounds.

Recordings and Sheet Music

Seder Melodies. Tara Publications, 1997. Velvel Pasternak and a children's choir sing *Pesach* songs; with transliterated Hebrew.

Songs of the Haggadah. Tara Publications, 1997. Music from the *Haggadah*, music book, and cassette.

Video Tapes

The Animated Haggadah. Scopus Films, 1985. A delightful clay animation of the *Pesach* story.

The Four Sons: A Guide to Passover. Ergo Media, 1988. Theodore Bikel stars as a delicatessen owner explaining *Pesach.*

The Joy of Passover: How to Create One Passover Seder You'll Never Forget. Institute for Creative Jewish Media, 1987. Explanations, how to prepare foods, lists of supplies.

Lambchop's Passover Stories. CTP Youngheart, n.d. Shari Lewis and her puppets celebrate Passover.

Passover: Jerusalem Jones and the Lost Afikomen. Children's Television Workshop, 1991. Kippi and Jerusalem Jones leap into the pages of the *Haggadah.*

Passover: Traditions of Freedom. Maryland Public Television, 1994. Traditional and ethnic worldwide celebrations of Passover; Israel and the United States.

A Passover Adventure. Israel Instructional Television Centre, 1984. American-born Israeli in Egypt; *Pesach* customs throughout Israel.

Passover at Bubbe's. Pan-Imago and Jean Doumanian Productions, 1990. Bubbe (grandmother) gets lots of help preparing for *Pesach;* travel to ancient Egypt.

A Passover Seder. Kid Vision, 1994. Presented by Elie Wiesel; includes his personal memories; many generations of a family celebrating the holiday.

Shalom Sesame Passover: Jerusalem Jones and the Lost Afikoman. Sisu Home Entertainment, 1991. The Sesame Street characters celebrate Passover.

Notes on Sources

Some parts of this book come from the Torah—the first five books of the Bible—and from other parts of the Bible as well. Other parts of the book come from the Babylonian Talmud, a sacred text that explains or interprets the Bible. And other parts come from the *midrash,* stories that the Rabbis in *Eretz Yisrael* wrote almost two thousand years ago to explain passages in the Bible.

The four places in the Torah that instruct parents to tell the Passover story to their children are from Exodus 12:26; Exodus 13:3 and 13:8; and Deuteronomy 6:20–21.

Introduction

The Book of Exodus 13:4 tells us that the Children of Israel left Egypt in the spring.

Chapter 1

The story of the Exodus from Egypt comes from the Book of Exodus in the Torah. Every week on Shabbat we read a portion of the Torah, and each portion has its own name. The parts that tell the Exodus story are called *Shemot, Va'era, Bo,* and *Beshalach.* These are the portions that Barbara and Cherie used in their retelling of the Exodus story.

The ancient Rabbis wrote many *midrashim* about stories in the Book of Exodus. The collection of these *midrashim* is called *Exodus Rabbah.* In *Exodus Rabbah* you will find the story of Miriam's dream, the story of baby Moses and the glowing coal, and the story of Miriam teaching Moses about his heritage. Miriam's dream is also in the Talmud section called *Sotah.* The Miriam story in this book is in chapter 3.

The *midrashim* "Fruits from the Sea" and "Taking Risks" are also from *Exodus Rabbah.* The story of Nachshon jumping first into the Red Sea is told in the Talmud section Sotah and in *midrash.*

The Queen of Sheba/King Solomon riddles are found in *Midrash Mishle* I, 20–21, 40–41, and *Midrash HaHefetz.*

Chapter 2

Rabbi Akiba's discussion about the frog is from the Talmud: B. Sanh. 67b.

Chapter 3

The part that tells about Adam and Eve and the spices comes from *midrash* and can be found in *Genesis Rabbah.* Information about the brave women of Egypt and about the midwives is in *Exodus Rabbah* and in the Talmud section *Sotah.* The story of Miriam's Well is in *midrashim* that explain the Torah *and* other parts of the Bible. These are *Numbers Rabbah* 1:2 and *Song of*

Songs Rabbah 4:12. The reference to the women taking jewelry is from the Torah (Exodus 3:22).

Chapter 5

Our explanation of the Ashkenazic, Sephardic, and Oriental Jews was formulated with the help of Professor Dov Noy, founder of the Israel Folktale Archives.

Chapter 8

We are commanded to eat *matzah* in the Book of Exodus 12:15.

Chapter 9

The four ways that God will save the Children of Israel are from Exodus 6.

Some stories in our book were told by people who heard them in their own families. Most of these stories are in the Israel Folktale Archives (IFA) in Haifa, Israel. This archive is a collection of more than 22,000 stories, told by Jews who now live in Israel and who have come from almost every country in the world where Jews have lived. Every story has its own IFA number.

"*Dayenu*" (chapter 10) was told by Chimon Hillel who came from Tunisia. The IFA number is 1311. Part of the story was told to Meir Noy by his father in Galicia, which was part of Poland; IFA number 7812.

"The Treasured Cup of Elijah" (chapter 13) was told by Nehemya Varenbod from the Ukraine; IFA number 10819.

"The *Matzah* Cover That Saved a Life" (chapter 8) was told by Avraham Urmoza from Syria; IFA number 8563.

"A Letter to God" (chapter 5) was told by Baruch Zarabi from Iran; IFA number 5519.

The Ethiopian story (chapter 14) was told by Moshe Taazazo of Ethiopia; IFA number 14,873.

"The *Haggadah* that Traveled" (chapter 6) was told by Fred Hertz to Barbara Rush. It is not an IFA story.

Some of the stories created by Barbara and Cherie were inspired by other stories. "Elijah's Passover Return" was inspired by a story written by Tsila Cohen. "Hershele's Passover Feast" and "Passover Clothing in Chelm" were inspired by classic stories of Hershele and of Chelm. "Jerusalem's Secret" was inspired by a legend that was told to Barbara by Moses Aaron, a storyteller from Australia. "Radishes for the Seder" is based on a story that Barbara heard thirty-five years ago when she was a teacher at Temple Israel in New Rochelle, N.Y. "Miriam and Her Tambourine" and the froggy story-poem are Cherie's and Barbara's own *midrashim*.

Haggadot Used in This Book

Title page in Hebrew.
Geismar Haggadah, Germany, 1928

A Note on Haggadot

Thousands and thousands of *Haggadot* have been produced over hundreds of years from many, many countries. Each *Haggadah* is known by a special name. Some *Haggadot* are named after the city where they were written (like the Jerusalem *Haggadah* from Israel). Other *Haggadot* were named for the artist (like the Geismar *Haggadah,* with pictures by Otto Geismar). And sometimes a *Haggadah* is named for the publisher (like the Eisenstein *Haggadah* from New York). If there are many *Haggadot* made in a place (like Livorno, Italy), then the date is also given in its name.

From the Collection of Dr. Herbert E. Wollowick

Aleppo *Haggadah,* Syria, 1897; very rare; kabbalistic influences; Hebrew and Judaic-Arabic.

Bombay (Bene Israel) *Haggadah,* India, 1846; in Marathi and Hebrew; one of the earliest Indian *Haggadot.*

Cairo *Haggadah,* Egypt, 1931; Arabic script and Hebrew.

Eisenstein *Haggadah,* New York, 1928; Lola: illustrator; published by Hebrew Publishing Company.

Fürth *Haggadah,* Fürth, Germany, 1774; rare *Haggadah;* Hebrew and Yiddish.

Geismar *Haggadah,* Berlin, Germany, 1928; Otto Geismar: editor and illustrator.

Jerusalem *Haggadah,* 1863; rare; commentaries by major rabbis.

Livorno *Haggadah,* Italy, 1867; Sephardic; Hebrew, and Ladino translation.

Livorno *Haggadah,* Italy, 1887; produced for Arabic countries with Hebrew and Judeo-Arabic translations.

Poona (Bene Israel) *Haggadah,* India, 1874; writing in Marathi and Hebrew.

Prague *Haggadah,* Czechoslovakia, 1777; extremely rare; only two copies are known to exist.

Prague *Haggadah,* Czechoslovakia, 1784; Yiddish translations from Hebrew.

Sousse *Haggadah,* Tunisia, 1948; in three languages: Hebrew, Judeo-Arabic, and French.

Venice *Haggadah,* Italy, 1792; Sephardic rite.

Verona *Haggadah,* Italy, 1828; used in Corfu, Greece; Sephardic rite; pictures from Venice *Haggadah,* early seventeenth century (earliest known *Haggadah* illustrations).

Other Haggadot Used in This Book

Budapest *Haggadah,* Hungary; twentieth century.

Hertz Family *Haggadah,* Roedelheim, Germany, 1918; published as *Hagadah: Erzaehlung von dem Auszuge Iraels aus Aegypten* by M. Lehrberger and Co.; Hebrew and German.

Title page in German.
Geismar Haggadah, Germany, 1928

Bibliography

Books We Used for Research in Writing Our Book

Avital, Samuel. *The Passover Haggadah*. NOTE: Private printing. Avital compiled, arranged, and gave commentary in this edition.

Ben-Ya'akov, Abraham. "Mi Minhagim Shiftey Israel." In *The Customs of the Tribes of Israel*. Israeli Ministry of Education, 1967.

Berman, Melanie. *Sharing Passover: A Guide to Celebrating with Your Kids*. New York: Comet International Inc., 1994.

Bronner, E. M. with Naomi Nimrod. *The Women's Haggadah*. San Francisco: Harper San Francisco, 1993.

Chaikin, Miriam. *Ask Another Question: The Story and Meaning of Passover*. New York: Clarion Books (Ticknor and Fields: A Houghton Mifflin Co.), 1985.

Cohen, Jeffrey, M. *1001 Questions and Answers on Pesach*. Northvale, N.J.: Jason Aronson, 1996.

Drucker, Malka. *Passover: A Season of Freedom*. New York: Holiday House, 1981.

Elias, Rabbi Joseph. *The Haggadah*. Artscroll Mesorah Series. New York: Mesorah Pub., Ltd., 1977, 1978, 1980, 1989.

Fluek, Toby Knobel with Lillian Fluek Finkler. *Passover as I Remember It*. New York: Alfred A. Knopf, 1994.

Freedman, Jacob, DD. *Polychrome Historical Haggadah for Passover*. Springfield, Ma.: JF Liturgy Research Foundation, 1974.

Fredman, Ruth Gruber. *The Passover Seder: Afikomen in Exile*. Philadelphia: University of Pennsylvania Press, 1981.

Gaster, Theodor H. *Passover: Its History and Traditions*. New York: Henry Shuman, Inc., 1949.

———. *Festivals of the Jewish Year*. Woodmere, N.Y.: William Morris Society, 1972.

Geffen, David. *American Heritage Haggadah: The Passover Experience*. Jerusalem: Geffen Pub. House, 1992.

Glatzer, Nahum M., ed. *The Passover Haggadah*. New York: Schocken Books, 1953, 1969.

Goodman, Philip. *The Passover Anthology*. Philadelphia: Jewish Publication Society of America, 1973.

Hacohen, Rabbi Menachem. *The Passover Haggadah: Legends and Customs*. New York: Adama Books, 1987.

Kaplan, Mordecai M., Eugene Kohn, and Ira Eisenstein, eds. *The New Haggadah for the Pesah Seder*. West Orange, N.J.: Behrman House, 1942, 1978.

Kibbutz Givat Brenner. *Haggadah for Passover*. Kibbutz Givat Brenner, Israel, 1964.

Kolatch, Rabbi Alfred J. *The Family Seder: A Traditional Passover Haggadah for the Modern Home*. New York: Jonathan David Pub., 1967.

Kramer, Ralph M. and Philip Schild. *The Bay Area Jewish Forum Haggadah*. This book was originally self-published by the authors in the San Francisco Bay Area, 1986. Revised edition, Berkley: Benmir Books, 19__.

Levin, Meyer. *An Israel Haggadah for Passover*. New York: Harry Abrams, Inc., n.d.

Levy, Rabbi Richard N. *On Wings of Freedom: The Hillel Haggadah for the Nights of Passover*. Hoboken, N.J.: B'nai Brith Hillel Foundations/Ktav Pub. House, 1989.

Nathan, Joan. *Jewish Cooking in America*. New York: Alfred A. Knopf, 1994.

Noy, Dov. *Cantes Populaire Racontes par des Juifs de Tunisie* (Popular tales told by the Jews of Tunisia). Israel Folktale Archives, 1968.

Noy, Meir. *Sipur U'Minhagim Bo* (East European Jewish cante fables). Israel Folktale Archives, 1968.

Paley, Grace. (Preface) *The Shalom Seders: Three Haggadahs Compiled by the New Jewish Agenda*. New York: Adama Books, 1984.

Pasternak, Velvel. *The International Jewish Songbook*. Cedarhurst, New York: Tara Publications, 1994.

Rabinowicz, Rachel Anne, ed. *Passover Haggadah: The Feast of Freedom*. New York: The Rabbinical Assembly, 1982.

Raphael, Chaim. *A Feast of History: Passover through the Ages as a Key to Jewish Experience*. New York: Simon and Schuster, 1972.

Riskin, Rabbi Shlomo. *The Passover Haggadah*. New York: Ktav Publishing House, Inc., 1983.

Ross, Lesli Koppelman. *Celebrate: The Complete Jewish Holidays Handbook*. Northvale, N.J.: Jason Aronson Publishers, 1994.

Schauss, Hayyim. *The Jewish Festivals: History and Observance*. New York: Schocken Books, 1962.

Silberman, Shoshana. *A Family Haggadah*. Rockville, Md.: Kar-Ben Copies, Inc., 1987.

Strassfeld, Michael. *A Passover Seder*. New York: The Rabbinical Assembly, 1979.

Wolfson, Ron, Dr. with Joel Lurie Grishaver. *The Art of Jewish Living: The Passover Seder*. Book, teacher's manual, and implementation guide. New York: The Federation of Jewish Men's Clubs, 1988 with the University of Judaism.

Acknowledgments

Writing this Passover book has been a wondrous trip through time and place. We have met, talked to, and shared stories with many, many people: from family to friends, to new friends around the world, who have opened our eyes and hearts to endless ways to celebrate Passover, both ancient and modern. Our list overflows the page, and our gratitude to them overwhelms us. May their (and your!) Elijah and Miriam Cups be ever-flowing and overflowing with abundant blessings of peace, freedom, and creativity! Amen, sela!

Our special gratitude and many, many thanks to:

Bruce Black, our editor at The Jewish Publication Society, whose vision and wise counsel, whose humor and infinite patience, whose belief in us and in this project helped shape this book in beauty during its long birthing!

Special thanks to the JPS editor-in-chief, Ellen Frankel, copy editors Christine Sweeney and Sydelle Zove, consultant Rabbi Israel Stein, and the JPS production staff.

The Amado Foundation, whose support of this project and its worldwide scope, and whose generous financial contribution made the publication of this book possible.

Dr. Herbert E. Wollowick, collector of over 700 *Haggadot* from around the world dating back hundreds of years, for his *Haggadah* knowledge and his support; and his gracious permission for us to use the many beautiful *Haggadah* illustrations for this book. (This story began with Cherie meeting Herb on an AJC Morocco trip!) Our book is indeed enriched by his contributions.

Don Rush and Larry Schwartz, our incredibly supportive, technology-and-computer-minded husbands, who guided us through the creation of this whole book with such patience and care, and who even participated via photography and art!

Dotty Karo, Cherie's mom, for advice, love, and support; and for many recipes and crafts.

Child author Rachel Sara Petroff, age 11, for her original story.

A whole wide world of many, many thanks to:

Professor Dov Noy of the Hebrew University, Jerusalem, founder of the Israel Folktale Archives, for his boundless knowledge of folklore and his support; and for his explanation of Ashkenazic, Sephardic, and Oriental Jews;

Professor Aliza Shenhar and Ms. Edna Hechal, and the Israel Folktale Archives in Haifa, Israel, for help in locating stories, and permission to print them;

Dr. Eli Marcus for folklore information;
Dr. Sheva Zucker for Yiddish information;
Dr. Regina Igel for historic information;
Professor Howard Schwartz for his support, wisdom, and knowledge; and
Rabbi Israel C. Stein for his careful review of the manuscript.

For all the extra help and support, hearty thanks to:

Pearl Lam, Joyce Karriko, and the Jewish Braille Institute of America for information on and examples of Hebrew Braille;

The American Printing House for the Blind for Braille translations;

Library of The Colorado Agency for Jewish Education, Denver Colo.; Librarian: Bernice Tarlie;

Library of Temple Emanuel, Denver Colo.; Librarian: Susan Berson;

The Rosenzweig Museum of the Jewish Family at Judea Reform Congregation, Durham, N.C., and to Dr. Lenora Ucko, curator, for permission to photograph these treasures of the museum: the *Chad Gadya* page from the Budapest *Haggadah;* "Next Year in Jerusalem" on a printed hand towel from Germany in the 1800s; a silver Elijah's Cup from Czechoslovakia;

Rabbi John Friedman and Abby Friedman, Judea Reform Congregation, Durham, N.C., for support and advice;

Bob and Barbara Jacobson and Ingrid Hertz for technical assistance;

Eve Kedem, principal of Judea Reform Congregation School, Durham, N.C., for use of the library;

Rabbi Brant Rosen, B'nai Havurah Reconstructionist Congregation, Denver, Colo., for support and advice; and for his explanation of redemption;

Dr. Dov Gavish, of the Hebrew University, for locating information and photographs; and

State of Israel, Central Bureau of Statistics.

For artists who bring our words to life, thanks with a flair to:

Judy Lande Haran, Butterfly Studios, Greensboro, N.C., an artist with exquisite vision: Our immense gratitude for the beautiful interwoven drawings that appear at the beginning of each section and throughout this book.

And to the other adult artists and photographers, thanks with a flair to:

Amy Cohen: photo of the *matzah* cover; photo of Ethan Cohen;

Joan Cohen: creator of the stenciled tablecloth design and the clay Miriam's Cup;

Foreign Office, State of Israel: photos of immigrants;

Vicky Hertz: photo of the *charoset* pyramid;

Dotty Karo: Froggy Critter, Miriam's Tambourine, Immigration Bookmarks, *Afikoman* bag;

Barbara Lehman, Lehman Design, Denver, Colo.: rubber stamp of Miriam dancing;

Helen Marks and Noah Hertz Marks: Seder Invitation craft;

Freya Mechanic: Jerusalem craft;

Lisa Rauchwerger, Cutting Edge Creations, Cleveland, Ohio: illuminated manuscript letter "Pey";

Sonia Rose: Exodus dolls;

Don Rush: North Carolina, New York, and California photographs;

Cherie Karo Schwartz: the Colorado photographs;

Larry Schwartz: many fine drawings;

Simha Shemesh: Moroccan clothing;

Rowanne Spector: for the idea that led to the Elijah peace-mat project;

Sue Speier: drawing of blue ribbon;

Dr. Herbert E. Wollowick: photos of *shmureh matzot;*

Pearl Wolfson, with her adult grandson, Geoff Wolfson: Hebrew calligraphy;

For the young artists whose drawings grace these pages, a dor l'dor todah to:

Zak, Lucy, and Aaron Schwartz (grandchildren extraordinaire!), Denver, Colo.: immensely talented artists whose many creative drawings appear throughout our book;

Seth and Cheryl Rush, (grandchildren extraordinaire!), Commack, N.Y.;

Ishayah Waters and Shoshanah Grace, (grandchildren extraordinaire!), Redway, CA;

Artists from the Chattanooga Jewish Community Religious School, Chattanooga, Tenn.: Stephanie Hays and Ben Solovey; Teacher: Amy Cohen;

Artists from the Herzl Day School, Denver, Colo.: Leah Glass, Coby Gould, Rebecca Reiman, and Lucy Wohlauer; Teacher: Sheila Silverman;

Artists from the Jewish Community Day School, Durham, N.C.: Second-grade artist Katherine Leibel; and the kindergarten class; Principal: Simone Soltan and Judaic Studies Teacher: Rachel Ariel;

Ilana Blumenfeld-Gantz, Harrison, N.Y.;
Chapin Campbell, Chapel Hill, N.C.;
Ethan Cohen, Chattanooga, Tenn.;
Yoni Dinur, Givat Ze'ev, Israel;
Rosie and Sally Jablonsky, Spokane, Wash.;
Noah Hertz Marks, Chapel Hill, N.C.;
Melody and O.J. Mechanic, Seattle, Wash.; and
Brian Raphael, Sanford, N.C.
Lauren Jennifer Staub, DeWitt, N.Y.

For cooking projects, sweet thanks to:

Dotty Karo, Cherie's mom: recipes for Sweet Israel Chicken, *matzo* balls, *charoset* (from her mother, Rae Olesh, from England), Forgotten Cloud Cookies;

Joan Cohen: her *charoset* recipe;
Vicky Hertz: for her *charoset* pyramid recipe;
Seemah Mares: for her Rangoon *charoset* recipe;
Goldie Rushefsky: for recipe refinement; and
Heinz and Kurt Speier: for their Passover cake recipe.

For music help, thanks of note to:

Fran Avni for the blessing of her voice and her friendship, and for her original musical contributions, which help give our stories life in this book;

Linda Hirschhorn for the strength and beauty of her music, and for the Miriam song in this book;

Eugene and Atarah Jablonsky for transcribing music; and

Velvel Pasternak, founder of Tara Publications, and his son, Mayer, for their vast musical knowledge, and for permission to print traditional Passover songs from Velvel's book, *The International Jewish Songbook*.

For sharing special family customs, traditional thanks to:

Dr. Ada Aharoni (Egypt);
Doron Elia (Romania);
Tziporah Sibahi Greenfield (Yemen);
Fred Hertz (Germany);
Azariah Levy (Iran);
Simone Lipman (Alsace);
Rabbi Zalman Schachter-Shalomi and Eve Ilsen (United States);
Peninnah Schram (Lithuania);

Simha Shemesh (Morocco);
Eliot Spack and family (United States); and
Emile Zafrany (Morocco).

For all of the friends and relatives who posed for photos, thanks with a flash to:

Zoë and Anna Aqua, ages 8 and 5, Colorado;
Pearl Auerbach, Colorado and Florida;
Brooke and Lauren Brown, ages 6 and 9, North Carolina;
Aliza, Geoffrey, and Ethan Cohen, ages 1 ½, 9, and 8, Tennessee;
Danielle Cohen, age 3 ½, North Carolina;
Matan Goodkind, age 5, California;
Shoshanah Grace, age 7, California;

Abraham Hebrew and Family, Pakistan and California;

Aaron Hertz, age 14, North Carolina;

Jonathan Kaufman, age 13, Pennsylvania;

Benna and Mira Kessler, ages 4 ½ and 11, North Carolina;

Ronda Mangham, Colorado;

Noah, Samuel, and Benjamin Hertz Marks, ages 9, 7, and 3 ½ North Carolina;

Alison and Steven Moss, ages 5 ½ and 2, Colorado;

Ellen Peiper, age 11, North Carolina;

Lewis, Megan, and Sam Romer, ages 12 and 8 (Megan and Sam), North Carolina;

Seth and Cheryl Rush, ages 11 and 9, New York;

Julia, Sari, and Spencer Schulman, ages 8, 13, and 11, North Carolina;

Jeremy and Zak Susel, ages 12 and 10, Colorado; and

Ishayah Waters, age 9, California.

Index

Aaron (brother of Moses), 6, 12

Aba Mahari, the Cohen, 166

Abraham (patriarch), 4

activities: bar/bat mitzvah trip to Israel, 179; Elijah buddies, 160–61; family treasures, 173–74; gardening, 15; gathering family stories, 171–72; "interviewing" Pharaoh, 26; Israel exhibits, 179–80; nature walk, 15; new "Dayenu," 121; pen pals, 178–79; prayer for Jerusalem, 182–83; recycling, 140; sharing *matzot,* 99; spring cleaning, 58; writing poems, 15–16. *See also* crafts projects; games; recipes

"Adir Hu" (traditional song), 184–85

Afghanistan, customs from, 83

afikoman: breaking of, 91, 99–100; eating of, 91–92, 142; hiding of, 91, 100–101, 147–48; questions about, 147–48; searching for, 142, 149–51

afikoman bag (crafts), 146–47

aggadot (stories), 62

Aharoni, Dr. Ada, 13–14, 170, 182

Akiba (rabbi), 18

almond cake (recipe), 136–38

American Joint Distribution Committee (JDC), 99

American Sign Language (ASL), 47

Amram, 5

Ashkenazic (Ashkenazi) Jews, xxii

"Avadim Hayinu" (traditional song), 45

Baal Shem Tov, 158

"Baby Moses" (Avni), 10

Balkans, customs in, 75

Barech (grace), 73

bedikat chametz ("searching for chametz"), 57

besamim, 35

betzah (egg): recipes for, 83–84; symbolism of, 83

B'hatzlacha ("May you succeed!"), 108

Bible, defined, xxi. *See also* Torah

Biblical citations: Gen. 19, 114; Exod., 4–7; Exod. 3:22, 107; Exod. 12:15, 56–57; Exod. 14:31, 67; Exod. 15:20, 28; Is. 2:4, 193; Ps. 113, 163; Ps. 115, 163; Ps. 116, 163; Ps. 117, 163; Ps. 118, 163; Ps. 122:6-7, 181; Ps. 136, 122, 163

bimuelos, 131

Birkat Hamazon ("Blessing of the Food"), 73, 151

"B'ivhilut" (traditional song), 46–47

blessings: for the land, 17; at Passover, 72–73. *See also specific blessings and prayers*

Braille *Haggadot,* 63–64

b'seder *("It's okay"),* 73

Bukhara, customs from, 99–100, 107

Burmese *charoset* (recipe), 79–80

cake, almond (recipe), 136–38

caponata, 131

carrot top plants, 140

Caucasus Mountains, customs from, 85

"Cavritico, Un" (Ladino song), 190

celery trees, 140

"Chad Gadya" (traditional song), 189–91

Chag ha Aviv (Holiday of Spring), 3

Chag ha Matzot (Holiday of Matzah), 3

Chag ha Pesach (Holiday of Paschal Offering), 3

chametz (leavened foods): clearing away, 57–58, 59, 107; defined, 14, 51, 56–58

charoses/charoset (sweet mortar): recipes for, 76, 77–81; symbolism of, 76

Chelm, Poland, 104–6

chicken, sweet Israel (recipe), 135–36

Children of Israel, defined, xxi

chol ha'moed ("in between days"), 74

Civil War, 99

clay figures (crafts), 167

clothing, 104–6, 107

clouds, pillar of, 6

Cohen, Danielle, 78

compote, 128

conversion, forced, 69–72, 107

cookies (recipe), 138–39

crafts projects: *afikoman* bag, 146–47; Chad Gadya glove, 191; clay figures, 167; Elijah's cup, 161–62; Exodus mural, 8–9; freedom banner, 42–43; froggy critter, 20–23; illuminated *Haggadah* pages, 66–67; immigration bookmarks, 174–75; immigration tiles, 167; Jerusalem puzzle, 180; *kippah,* 113; *matzah* cover, 95–96; micrography picture, 122–23; Miriam's tambourine, 31; papercut *mizrach,* 180–82; plague puppetry, 24–25; seder invitations, 55–56; seder plate symbols tablecloth, 85–88; welcome blessing placemat, 163

Crossing of the Red Sea. *See* Red (Reed) Sea, crossing of

cup (of wine), for Elijah, 146, 156, 158, 161–62

David, King of Israel, 176

"Dayenu" (traditional song), 116–21

dietary laws. *See chametz* (leavened foods)

Eastern Europe: *charoses* from (recipe), 77; *matzah* balls from, 124

eggplant, spicy (recipe), 134–35

Egypt: Exodus from, 3, 4–7; modern emigration from, 169–70

"Ehad Mi Yodei-a" (traditional song), 186–87

Elia, Doron, 170

Elijah the Prophet, 113, 142–46, 154–63

"Eliyahu ha Navi" (traditional), 146, 159

Ellis Island, 172

English *charoses* (recipe), 78

Eretz Yisrael, immigration to, 167–68

Esther, Queen of Persia, 37

Ethiopia, exodus from, 164, 165–66

Exodus (from Egypt): and freedom, 38–41; *midrashim* about, 11–13; story of, 3, 4–7

exoduses, recent, 164–66, 167–68, 169–71

famine, 4

fire, pillar of, 6

food. *See matzah;* rice; seder plate; seders, festive meal during

forgotten cookie clouds (recipe), 138–39

four, occurrences of, 113–15

Four Questions: changes in, 112; customs about, 109, 110; song for, 111–12; symbolism of, 108–9

Four Sons, 114–15

France, customs from, 58, 83

freedom, 38–49

frittata, 131

frogs, plague of, 18–20

"Frogs and More Frogs" (poem), 19–20

games: with nuts, 81; packing for the Exodus, 14; searching for *chametz,* 58. *See also* puzzles; riddles

gardening, 15, 140

gefilte fish, 128

gemilut chasadim (deeds of loving kindness), 160–61

Germany, survival of *Haggadah* in, 60–62

Gibraltar, customs from, 75

Glick, Hirsch: "Hymn of the Partisans," 43

Greenfield, Ziporah Sibahi, 169

Haggadah: for the blind, 63–64; description of, 60–62, xvi; meaning of, 62; *midrashim* in, 11; oldest, 63; reading of, 62–63; women not mentioned in, 28

Haggadah, illustrations from: Aleppo *Haggadah,* 86; Amsterdam *Haggadah,* 57; Bombay *Haggadah,* 86; Budapest *Haggadah,* 190; Cairo *Haggadah,* 18; Eisenstein *Haggadah,* 19, 66, 189, 191; Geismar *Haggadah,* 4, 5, 6, 25, 28, 36, 49, 109, 151; Jerusalem *Haggadah,* 176; Livorno *Haggadah,* 7, 109; Mantua *Haggadah,* 154; Poona *Haggadah,* 96; Prague *Haggadah,* 115; Sousse *Haggadah,* 86; Verona *Haggadah,* 63, 90

Hallel ("praise"), 73, 163

hamsa (hand) seder plate, 89

Hasidic Jews, 158

Havdalah, 35

Hebrew language, xxiii

Hebrews, defined, xxi

Hertz, Fred, 60

Hertz, Vicky, 80

Herzl, Theodor, 170

Hillel sandwich (Korech), 73, 76

"History" (Avni), 65

Holland, customs from, 158

Holocaust, seders during, 75

horseradish, 75, 76

"Hymn of the Partisans" (Glick), 43

hyssop, 74

illuminated manuscripts, 66–67

Ilsen, Eve, 130

immigration bookmarks, 174–75

invitations, 54–56

Iran (Persia): customs from, 123; folktale from, 52–54

Iraq, customs from, 99–100

Isaac, 4

Israel: bar/bat mitzvah trip to, 179; forty-year journey to, 7; immigration to, 164, 167–68, 169–71; local exhibits about, 179–80; number of seders in, 74; pen pals from, 178–79

Israelites, defined, xxi

Italian rice soup (recipe), 131–32

Jacob, 4

Jerusalem: construction of, 176; *L'shanah Ha'ba'ah B'Yerushalayim* ("Next year in Jerusalem"), 146, 176–83; pilgrimages to, 176; story about, 177–78

Jewish Braille Institute of America, 64

Jews: defined, xxi; killing of baby boys decreed, 5; killing of the firstborn decreed, 6; types of, xxii

Joseph, 4

Judeo-Arabic language, xxiii

Judeo-German language, 61

Judeo-Persian language, 106–7, xxiii

Judeo-Spanish language. *See* Ladino language

Kadesh, 73

k'arah (seder plate), 68. *See also* seder plate

Karaite Jews, 124

karpas (greens): blessing of, 73; symbolism of, 74–75

keffiyahs, 107

kibbutzim, seders at, 16

kiddush (blessing of the wine), 72, 73

kippah (head covering), 113

knaidlach (*matzo* balls) (recipe), 124, 128–31

Korech (Hillel sandwich), 73, 76

kos Miryam (Miriam's cup), 35

Kristallnacht, 60

Kurdistan, customs from, 99, 107

Ladino language, 170, 186, 188, 190, xxiii

languages, 47, xxii–xxiii

Leah (matriarch), 37

l'sa-der ("to straighten out"), 73

Levy, Azariah, 123

l'hagid ("to tell"), 62

Libya, customs from, 83

Lipman, Simone, 58, 131

Lithuania, customs from, 130

Lot, Passover celebrated by, 114

"*Lo Yisa Goy*" (traditional song), 193–95

"*L'shanah Haba-ah Biy'rushalayim*" (traditional song), 183

L'shanah Ha'ba'ah B'Yerushalayim ("Next year in Jerusalem"), 146, 176–83

Maggid, 73

maggid (one who teaches through stories), 62

"*Mah Nishtanah*" (traditional song), 111–12

Maimuna, 193

ma'ot chittim (ma'os chittim), 98

Mares, Seemah, 79

maror (bitter herbs): blessing of, 73; symbolism of, 75–76

Matriarchs, 37

matzah: blessing of, 73; customs for, 98, 99–101; description of, 90, 97, 124; recipe for, 96–97; sharing of, 99; symbolism of, 48, 90–92

matzah covers: creating your own, 95; symbolism of, 91, 92–94

Matzah of Hope, 101

matzo balls *(knaidlach),* 124, 128–31

matzo brei, 192

matzo farfel kugel, 128

Meir, Golda, 37

micrography, 122–23

Midian, 6

midrashim: creating your own, 30; defined, 11, xxi; about the Exodus, 11–13; about Miriam's tambourine, 29–30; about the ten plagues, 18–19

midwives, disobedience of, 37

mina, 131

minhagim (customs), 101, xviii

Miriam (sister of Moses): customs about, 35; dreams of, 11–12; Exodus celebrated (with tambourine) by, 7, 28, 29–30; Moses instructed by, 12; Moses saved by, 5, 11–12, 28, 36

"Miriam's Slow Snake Dance by the Riverside" (Hirschhorn), 31–34

Miriam's Well, 30, 35

mirrors, turning to the wall, 106

Mitzrayim (Egypt), defined, 4, xxi

mitzvot (commandments), 16, 154, 165

mizrachim, 180–82

Morocco: customs from, 27, 46–47, 75, 83–84, 99, 107, 109, 193; recipes from, 132–33

Moses: age of, 107; birth of, 5; and the burning bush, 6; crossing the Red Sea, 7, 39–40, 41; God's instructions to, 6; Jewish identity of, 12; saved by Pharaoh's daughter, 5–6, 28; testing of, 12

Motzi Matzah (blessing), 73

music. *See* songs

Nachshon ben Aminadav, 13

nature walks, 15

Nehorai, Rabbi, 13

New Christians ("secret Jews"), 69–70, 107

Nirtzah, 73

Nisan, 3, 195

North Africa, customs from, 99–100, 109

Olesh, Rae (Rachel) Cohen, 78, 172

Operation Magic Carpet, 169

Oriental Jews, xxii

Ostropoler, Hershele, 125–28

Palestine. *See* Israel

parlsey, planting, 15

pasah ("to skip"), 3

Passover *(Pesach):* antiquity of, xxii; asking questions during, 104–15; people who celebrate it, xxii; reasons for celebrating, 3, 4–7; after the seder, 192–93. *See also Pesach*

Passover greetings, 106–7, 146, 182, 192, 193

pasta, 133

pastelicos, 131

pen pals, Israeli, 178–79

Persia. *See* Iran (Persia)

Pesach, defined, 3, xxi. *See also* Passover

Petroff, Rachel, 38

Pharaoh: "interview" with, 26; treatment of Jews by, 4–7

pillar of clouds, 6

pillar of fire, 6

plagues. *See* Ten Plagues

poems: about *afikoman,* 149–51; about frog plague, 19–20; about Jerusalem, 182–83; about seder plate, 85; about women, 36–37; writing for spring, 15–16

Poland, emigration from, 170–71

pomegranate seeds, 13–14

Portugal, customs from, 107, 192

projects. *See* activities

Puah (Egyptian midwife), 5, 28, 37
puppets, 24–25
Purim, 51
puzzles: about Jerusalem, 180; about
    Passover, 196; about the Ten
    Plagues, 25. *See also* riddles

"Quen Supiese" (traditional song), 186,
    188
questions. *See* Four Questions

Rachel (matriarch), 37
Rachtzah (blessing), 73
radishes. planting, 15, and seder plate,
    70–71
Rebecca (matriarch), 37
recipes: almond cake, 136–38; *charos
    es/charoset,* 76, 77–81; forgotten
    cookie clouds, 138–39; Italian rice
    soup, 131–32; *knaidlach (matzo
    balls),* 128–31; *matzah,* 96–97;
    Moroccan green soup, 132–33;
    red eggs, 83–84; spicy eggplant,
    134–35; sweet Israel chicken,
    135–36
recycling, 140
Redemption, defined, xxi
Red (Reed) Sea: crossing of, 7, 12–13,
    39–41; defined, xxi
Reed Sea. *See* Red Sea
resources (further reading), 198–203
rice, 124
riddles, 17, 59, 97–98
risk-taking, 13
Romania, emigration from, 170
Russia, *matzot* in, 99

sacrifices, 82–83
sadar (typesetter), 73

Samaritans: customs of, 107; foods of,
    133
Sarah (matriarch), 37
scallion "battles", 123
Schacter-Shalomi, Rabbi Zalman, 130
Schram, Peninnah, 130
seder plate, 68, 74–89; *betzah* (egg),
    83–84; *charoses/charoset* (sweet
    mortar), 76–81; creating a table-
    cloth of, 85–88; customs about,
    85; *hamsa* (hand) of, 89; *karpas*
    (greens), 74–75; *maror* (bitter
    herbs), 75–76; poem about, 85;
    seder talk about, 84; *zeroa*
    (shankbone), 82–83
seder readings: about freedom, 48;
    about women, 36–37
seders: blessings at, 72–73; celebra-
    tions during, 103–51; community-
    wide, 48–49; conclusion of,
    153–96; cost of, 52–54; descrip-
    tion of, 68; festive meal during,
    73, 124–41; finding one, 68–72;
    guests at, 54–55, 126–27; *at kib-
    butzim,* 16; new clothing for,
    104–6, 107; number of, 74; order
    of, 73; preparations for, 51–101;
    questions at, 104–6, 195; seder
    talk about, 73
seder talk: about blessings for the
    land, 17; about *chametz*-cleaning,
    59; about Elijah, 160; about end-
    ing the seder, 192; about exodus-
    es, 167–68; about the Four
    Questions, 112; about freedom,
    46, 47–48; about *Haggadot,*
    62–64, 67; about making things
    whole, 148–49; about *matzah,*
    97; about midwives, 37; about
    modern plagues, 27; about
    Moses, 67; about Passover memo-

ries, 141; about risk-taking, 13; about seder plate, 84; about seders, 73

Senesch, Hannah, 37

Sephardic (Sephardi) Jews, xxii

Shalosh Regalim, 176

shanda (Yiddish, disgrace), 130

Shavuot, 176

Shehekhiyanu (blessing), 72

Shemesh, Simha, 46, 132

Shifrah (Egyptian midwife), 5, 28, 37

Shmureh matzah, 90–91

Shomrei Adamah, 140

Shulhan Orech (festive meal), 73, 124–41

siddur (prayer book), 73

sidrah (weekly Torah portion), 73

Singapore, *charoset* from, 78–79

Solomon, King of Israel, 17, 176

songs: *"Adir Hu"* (traditional), 184–85; *"Avadim Hayinu"* (traditional), 45; "Baby Moses" (Avni), 10; *"B'ivhilut"* (traditional), 46–47; *"Chad Gadya"* (traditional), 189–91; *"Dayenu"* (traditional), 116–21; *"Ehad Mi Yodei-a"* (traditional), 186–87; *"Eliyahu ha Navi"* (traditional), 146, 159; at end of seder, 184–91, 193–95; Exodus rap, 11; "History" (Avni), 65; "Hymn of the Partisans" (Glick), 43; *"Lo Yisa Goy"* (traditional), 193–95; *"L'shanah Haba-ah Biy'rushalayim"* (traditional), 183; *"Mah Nishtanah"* (traditional), 111–12; "Miriam's Slow Snake Dance by the Riverside" (Hirschhorn), 31–34; *"Quen Supiese"* (traditional), 186, 188; "Wandering" (Avni), 44

Spack, Eliot, 101

Spain: customs from, 107, 192; expulsion of Jews from, 61; "secret Jews" in, 69–72, 107

Speier, Heinz and Kurt, 136, 138

spices, 35

spicy eggplant (recipe), 134–35

spring cleaning, 58

storytelling, 30, 119. *See also aggadot* (stories); *midrashim*

Sukkot, 176

sweet Israel chicken (recipe), 135–36

Syria, folktale from, 92–94

Taazazo, Moshe, 164

tablecloths, with seder plate symbols, 85, 87–89

Talmud: *chametz*-cleaning mentioned in, 57; *midrashim* in, 11; women mentioned in, 28, 36

Ten Plagues: crafts about, 20–25; customs about, 26–27; story of, 6, 18–19

Theodorus, Emperor of Ethiopia, 164, 165

tikkun olam, 149

Torah: defined, xxi; 613 commandments in, 14

tsimmes, 128

Tsipporah, 6

Tu B'Shevat, 15

Tzafun, 73

tzedakah (charity), 156, 157

Ukraine, folktale from, 155–57

U'rechatz, 73

visiting friends, 193

"Wandering" (Avni), 44
water, beating of, 192
Western Wall *(Kotel),* 176–77
wine: blessing of *(kiddush),* 72, 73;
    drinking cups of, 115; for Elijah,
    146; symbolizing the plagues,
    26–27
Wishengrad, Abraham, 170
women, honoring of, 28–37

Yachatz, 73
Yacov ben Yosef, 68–72

Yam-Suf. See Red (Reed) Sea
yarmulke, 113
Yemen: customs from, 75, 84–85, 107;
    emigration from, 169; seders in,
    63
Yiddish language, xxiii
Yocheved, 5, 28, 36

Zeman Cherutainu (Season of Our
    Freedom), 3
zeroa (shankbone), 82–83